# PLANT-BASED HIGH-PROTEIN DIET COOKBOOK

+50 EASY, HEALTHY AND DELICIOUS RECIPES FOR ATHLETIC PERFORMANCE AND MUSCLE GROWTH WITH LOW-CARB AND HIGH PROTEIN FOODS. NUTRITIONAL GUIDE FOR BEGINNERS TO EAT VEGGIE MEALS.

IRMA LOPEZ

# CONTENTS

# INTRODUCTION

More and more people are interested in following vegetarian or vegan diets or reducing their use of animal products. A shift away from animal products is getting easier with more fortified and nutritious plant-based foods available.

A person may try a vegan diet for health, animal welfare, or religious reasons. In 2016, the Academy of Nutrition and Dietetics stated that a vegetarian or vegan diet could provide all the nutritional requirements of adults, children, and those who were pregnant or breast-feeding.

Even so, getting enough protein and essential vitamins and minerals can be harder for people who do not eat meat or animal products. A person must plan ahead to ensure they get enough protein, calcium, iron, and vitamin B-12, which people on an omnivorous diet get from animal products.

**The Possible Benefits of Trading Meat Protein for Plant Protein**

One perk of eating animal protein is that these sources are complete — meaning they provide the nine essential amino acids our bodies can't make, according to the Cedars-Sinai Blog. But there are benefits to trading or reducing your meat consumption and filling up on plant proteins, including:

**Losing weight** When followed properly, plant-based diets, such as a vegetarian diet, may help you lose weight, according to a review of 12 randomized controlled trials published in January 2016 in the Journal of General Internal Medicine.

**Helping the environment** Swapping meat for plants to get your protein fix can similarly benefit the environment, notes an article published in December 2018 in Nutrients.

**Boosting your heart health** When it comes to red meat, the benefits of relying on plant alternatives for protein arguably get even more impressive. "Some studies have linked red meat with an increased risk of heart disease and type 2 diabetes, partly due to the saturated fat content," Sessions says.

In fact, a randomized controlled trial published in June 2019 in the American Journal of Clinical Nutrition found that among diets with red meat, diets with white meat, and diets with plants, the plant-based diets had the most positive effects on LDL or "bad" cholesterol levels. Per the American Heart Association, replacing saturated fat with healthier fats, such as polyunsaturated and monounsaturated fat, can benefit lipid and cholesterol levels.

Meanwhile, other research, like a meta-analysis published in April 2014 in JAMA Internal Medicine, reveals that compared with omnivorous dieters (those who eat both plant and animal proteins) vegetarians had lower diastolic and systolic blood pressure numbers. Those benefits can lead to a healthier ticker, lowering your risk for heart disease, according to the Centers for Disease Control and Prevention.

**Lengthening your life** The National Institutes of Health reports that red meat consumption may shorten your life. The group recommends swapping it out of your diet in favor of healthier protein sources.

By following a diet with a variety of foods, it's possible to get your fix of the amino acids your body needs to perform at its best.

# 1

# HABANERO CHEESE GRITS WITH PAN-BLACKENED FISH RECIPE

- Total Time: 50 min
- Prep Time: 30 min
- Cook Time: 20 min
- Servings: 4

Pan-blackening is an easy stovetop technique for preparing fish. Made with olive oil, as ours is, pan-blackening is a healthy alternative to deep-frying and can be used with any type of fish fillet.

Pan-blackened fish is paired here with spicy habanero cheese grits and with fresh vegetables to cool things down a bit. Pumpkin seeds and avocados can be included on a low-FODMAP diet when they are used as garnishes rather than main ingredients. Delicious!

## Ingredients

- 1 teaspoon smoked paprika
- 1 teaspoon ground cumin
- 1/2 teaspoon ground ancho chile
- 1/4 teaspoon ground mustard
- 1/4 teaspoon freshly ground black pepper
- 1/8 teaspoon ground cayenne pepper
- 1/8 teaspoon salt
- 1 pound cod or another firm white fish (four 4-ounce fillets)
- 2 1/4 cups reduced-sodium, low-FODMAP chicken broth (no garlic or onions)
- 1/2 cup uncooked corn grits
- 1/2 cup shredded habanero cheddar cheese, divided
- 2 tablespoons garlic-infused olive oil
- 4 cups thinly sliced Romaine lettuce
- 1 1/2 cups chopped fresh tomato
- 1/4 cup thinly sliced scallion greens (green part only)
- 1/2 medium avocado, chopped
- 3 tablespoons pumpkin seeds
- 3 tablespoons chopped cilantro
- 1 lime, in wedges

## Preparation

In a small bowl, combine paprika, cumin, ground chile, ground mustard, black pepper, cayenne pepper, and salt.

Sprinkle the spice mixture on both sides of each fish fillet. Spread the mixture evenly to the edges of each piece.

In a medium saucepan, stir together the chicken broth and grits; cover the pot. Over medium-high heat, bring the grits to a boil. Reduce the heat to maintain a simmer and cook the grits, stirring occasionally, until they are thickened and tender about 20 minutes. Remove pot from the heat, add half of the habanero cheddar, and stir until the cheese is melted.

While the grits are cooking, in a large cast iron or stainless steel skillet, warm the garlic-infused oil over medium-high heat. Once the oil in the pan is hot enough to sizzle a drop of water, add the fish fillets. Cook for 3 to 4 minutes, until thin edges become pale and opaque, then flip and cook for another 3 to 4 minutes. Check each fillet at its thickest point to be sure that it is done all the way through. Cooked fish is a solid white color and flakes apart easily. For best results, the entire surface of each fillet should make contact with the pan, so you may wish to cook the fish in two batches.

In each of 4 bowls, place a mound of cheese grits to one side. On the other side, arrange the lettuce and tomatoes. Top the vegetables with the cooked fish. To garnish, sprinkle each bowl with 1/4 of the remaining habanero cheddar, scallions, avocado, pumpkin seeds, and cilantro. Serve with wedges of lime.

Ingredient Variations and Substitutions: In addition to cod, thin fillets of tilapia, haddock, catfish, or sole can be used for this recipe. If you don't care for spicy food, substitute plain cheddar cheese for the habanero cheddar. For a dairy-free dish, omit the cheese. Instead stir 1/8 teaspoon crushed red pepper flakes into the grits, or more to taste.

**Cooking and Serving Tips**

Purchase fresh or "previously frozen" fish on the day you plan to serve it. If using frozen fish fillets, remove them from the freezer the night before and allow them to thaw in the refrigerator until it is time to prepare the meal.

Grits might take more or less time to cook, depending upon how finely they are ground. Defer to the cooking time suggested on product packaging, if available.

This recipe yields 4 s servings, each offering 3 ounces fish, 1/2 cup grits, and 1 3/4 cups salad.

**Nutrition Facts**

• Calories 410

- Total Fat 19g 24%
- Saturated Fat 5g 25%
- Cholesterol 75mg 25%
- Sodium 560mg 24%
- Total Carbohydrate 26g 9%
- Dietary Fiber 4g 14%
- Total Sugars 4g
- Includes 0g
- Added Sugars 0%
- Protein 36g

# LOW-FODMAP CHICKEN TIKKA MASALA RECIPE

- Total Time: 130 min
- Prep Time: 40 min
- Cook Time: 90 min
- Servings: 6 (3 oz. chicken, 1 cup sauce)

Chicken tikka masala begins with chunks of chicken marinated in a yogurt sauce. Traditionally, the chicken is then baked in a hot tandoori oven.

Our low-FODMAP version of this famous dish calls for broiling the chicken until it is nicely browned on the outside and still moist on the inside. Serve over long grain white or brown rice for the complete Indian restaurant experience.

**Ingredients**

- 1 tablespoon ground cumin
- 1 tablespoon paprika
- 2 teaspoons garam masala
- 1 teaspoon ground chile pepper
- 1 teaspoon ground turmeric
- 1/2 teaspoon ground coriander
- 1/2 teaspoon asafetida (see note below)
- 1/2 teaspoon freshly ground black pepper
- 1/2 teaspoon salt
- 1 1/2 cups lactose-free yogurt, divided
- 2 tablespoons minced, peeled fresh ginger root, divided
- 1 1/2 pounds boneless, skinless chicken breast
- 3 tablespoons garlic-infused olive oil
- 1 cup thinly sliced scallion greens (green part only)
- 2 cups chopped fennel bulb
- 2 cups thickly peeled, finely chopped fresh rutabaga
- 1 28-ounce can crushed tomatoes, no salt added
- 2 cups reduced-sodium, low-FODMAP chicken broth

**Preparation**

In a small bowl, mix together the cumin, paprika, garam masala, ground chile, turmeric, coriander, asafetida, black pepper, and salt. Divide this spice mixture in half and combine one half with a third of the yogurt and half of the minced ginger.

Cut chicken breasts into ½-inch thick fillets or tenders, so that they will cook properly under the broiler. Using a fork, poke holes in the surface of the chicken pieces to allow them to absorb more flavor. Place them in a large zip-top bag or flat dish, pour in the yogurt and spice mixture, seal, and refrigerate for 2 to 6 hours.

About 1½ hours before serving, heat a 4-quart saucepan or Dutch oven over medium heat. While the pan heats, add garlic-infused oil and the remaining minced ginger to the remaining half of the spice mixture; stir until this forms a thin paste. Add the paste to the hot pan and allow it to cook for 1 to 2 minutes until it is fragrant and darkens slightly. This is called "tempering" the spices.

Add the scallion greens, fennel bulb, and rutabaga and stir to coat with oil and spices. Sautee the vegetables until the scallion greens wilt, about 10 minutes. If the vegetables begin to stick, stir in a tablespoon of water.

Add the diced tomatoes and chicken broth. Stir to ensure that no vegetables are stuck to the bottom of the pan. Cover, bring to a low boil, then reduce heat to maintain a simmer for about 1 hour, stirring occasionally, until rutabaga is tender.

While the sauce simmers, arrange an oven rack about 4 inches below the broiler and preheat it.

Place the marinated chicken on an oiled or foil-lined broiling pan or baking tray. Place the chicken under the broiler for 3 to 4 minutes, until it begins to brown in spots. Remove the pan, turn the chicken pieces over, and broil on the other side until chicken is fully cooked. Remove smaller pieces of chicken from the broiling pan as they become done, to prevent over-cooking. Slice or cube the broiled chicken if desired.

Allow the sauce to cool for about 10 minutes until safe to handle. Use a stick blender to puree the sauce if desired or move it to a blender in batches. Stir in the rest of the yogurt and re-warm gently if necessary. Serve the chicken and sauce over cooked rice.

Ingredient Variations and Substitutions: To save time, serve the pieces of broiled chicken without slicing and serve the sauce without pureeing.

Three and a half cups of chopped fresh tomatoes can be used instead of the crushed tomatoes.

Cooking and Serving Tips: For the best flavor, plan ahead to start marinating the chicken early on the day you plan to serve this meal.

If you don't have garlic infused oil on hand, add a clove of garlic, cut into large pieces, to the oil when you temper the spices. Remove the pieces of garlic before adding the tomatoes and chicken broth.

Low-FODMAP chicken broth is one without onions or garlic. Be sure to read the ingredients label carefully before purchasing.

Asafetida, a spice used in traditional Indian cooking, adds an "allium" flavor note to this dish. Fortunately, it tastes much better than it smells. Try to borrow a small amount from a friend or buy just a little at first to make sure you like it. If you can't find it, omit it.

This sauce can be started well ahead of time. After cooking and pureeing it, refrigerate the sauce until shortly before serving. Re-warm it on the stovetop, then stir in the yogurt just before serving. Don't allow the yogurt to boil or it will curdle.

**Nutrition Facts**

- Calories 380
- Total Fat 13g 17%
- Saturated Fat 3g 15%
- Cholesterol 100mg 33%
- Sodium 540mg 23%
- Total Carbohydrate 23g 8%
- Dietary Fiber 6g 21%
- Total Sugars 14g
- Includes 0g Added Sugars 0%
- Protein 43g

# 3

# CALIFORNIA SUMMER VEGETABLE OMELET

- Total Time: 20 min
- Prep Time: 10 min
- Cook Time: 10 min
- Servings: 1

The best part of summer is all of the delicious fresh vegetables available at your local grocery store or the farmer's market. Vegetables are an important part of a healthy diet for blood pressure and disease prevention because of their fiber content, vitamins, potassium, magnesium, and antioxidants.

One of the easiest ways to add vegetables to your morning

meal is with an omelet. You can whip one up in under 20 minutes, or even *q*uicker if you chop your veggies the night before. This California summer vegetable omelet features fresh summer corn, zucchini, and tomatoes, along with flavorful cilantro and onion. Creamy avocado and a touch of cheese make it feel indulgent without making you sluggish. The combination of eggs, fresh vegetables, and avocado gives you lots of filling protein, healthy fat, and fiber—everything you need in a breakfast!

**Ingredients**

- Olive oil spray
- 1/4 cup zucchini, chopped
- 2 tablespoons onion, diced
- 1/4 cup cherry tomatoes, quartered
- 1/2 ear of corn, kernels removed and cob discarded
- 2 tablespoons cilantro, chopped
- 2 large eggs
- 1 tablespoon water
- Pinch black pepper
- 2 tablespoons monterrey jack cheese
- 1/4 small avocado, sliced

**Preparation**

Spray a small nonstick skillet with olive oil and heat on low.

Add zucchini and onion and cook, stirring, until onion is soft.

In a small bowl, mix tomatoes, corn kernels, and cilantro. Once zucchini mixture is cooked, remove from pan into bowl with corn mixture.

Wipe the skillet clean and spray with oil again. Place back on low heat.

In another small bowl, whisk together eggs, water, and pepper. Pour egg mixture into the skillet and let cook until eggs are almost set. You may cover the skillet to cook more quickly if your burner cooks hot.

Sprinkle corn mixture onto one half of the eggs. Top with

cheese and fold eggs in half over the vegetables and cheese. Continue cooking until eggs are fully set.

Carefully slide omelet from the pan onto a plate and top with sliced avocado.

Ingredient Variations and Substitutions: Remove or substitute vegetables to suit your preference. For lower fat or lower cholesterol, use egg whites or egg substitute.

Cooking and Serving Tips: To prevent burning, keep heat on low and cover skillet while eggs are cooking. Serve with whole grain toast and fruit to round out the meal.

**Nutrition Facts**

- Calories 319
- Total Fat 20g 26%
- Saturated Fat 7g 35%
- Cholesterol 385mg 128%
- Sodium 235mg 10%
- Total Carbohydrate 19g 7%
- Dietary Fiber 5g 18%
- Total Sugars 6g
- Includes 0g
- Added Sugars 0%
- Protein 19g

**4**

# VIETNAMESE VERMICELLI WITH CHILE SAUCE AND PORK RECIPE

- Total Time: 100 min
- Prep Time: 90 min
- Cook Time: 10 min
- Servings: 6

These noodle bowls are beautiful to behold, as well as a festival for the taste buds. They've got all the traditional southeast Asian flavors: sour, sweet, salty, and spicy. Even the temperatures of the ingredients are interesting.

Rice vermicelli are called "bun" in Vietnamese. Bun should be freshly cooked, yet cool, while the minced pork topping is warm.

The cooking techniques involved are actually very basic, making this special recipe within the reach of novice cooks, but do allow plenty of time for prepping the vegetables so you won't feel rushed. Recipes like this lend themselves to communal preparation—make it together with family or friends and then sit down to enjoy it together.

## Ingredients

- 10 tablespoons boiling water (1/2 cup plus 2 tablespoons)
- 2 tablespoons sugar
- ¼ cup fish sauce
- ¼ cup fresh lime juice (from 1 large lime)
- 2 small Thai chile peppers, fresh or dried
- 10 ounces uncooked rice vermicelli (bun)
- 4 cups lightly packed, torn romaine lettuce
- 3 cups fresh herb leaves, coarsely chopped (one or more: cilantro, Thai basil, mint)
- ½ English cucumber
- 2 ounces daikon radish
- 1 medium carrot
- 4 medium scallions
- 1 tablespoon peanut or canola oil
- 8 ounces lean ground pork
- 2 teaspoons sugar
- 1/4 teaspoon freshly ground black pepper
- ¾ cup chopped unsalted peanuts

## Preparation

Before you make the salad, start by prepping the sweet chili sauce. Grab a small bowl and stir together the boiling water, sugar, fish sauce, and lime juice until the sugar dissolves. Slice the chiles into paper-thin slices and stir them into the sauce.

In a large, covered stockpot, bring about 4 quarts of water to a rolling boil over high heat. Add the vermicelli and return the water to a boil, stirring gently several times to separate the block of vermicelli into strands. Begin testing for doneness after noodles have boiled about 2 minutes. When the vermicelli is tender, pour it into a strainer and rinse with cool water.

Divide the lettuce and herbs into 6 dinner-plate-sized bowls. Julienne the unpeeled cucumber, radish, and carrot, and divide among the bowls.

Slice the scallion greens and set them aside. Trim off the roots and cut the white part (bulb) of the scallions into large pieces.

In a medium skillet, heat the oil over medium heat. Add the scallion bulbs and allow the oil to infuse with their flavor as they cook. Adjust the heat to prevent burning, and remove the scallions when they begin to brown.

Add the ground pork and sugar and saute for 10 to 12 minutes, breaking it up into large pieces with a spatula, until browned.

Add 1/4 cup of the prepared sweet chile sauce to the skillet and stir, scraping the bottom of the pan, until it has evaporated. Remove from the heat and sprinkle with black pepper.

If necessary, loosen the vermicelli in the strainer by rinsing it again with some cold water. Arrange the noodles on top of the vegetables in the prepared bowls. Top each bowl with 1/6 of the ground pork, scallion greens, and chopped peanuts. Stir the sauce briskly and drizzle 2 1/2 tablespoons over each bowl. Serve immediately.

Ingredient Variations and Substitutions: Vary the herbs according to availability and your preferences. Dried herbs cannot be used instead of fresh since they serve as part of the salad greens, not just as seasonings.

Mung bean sprouts can be substituted for an equal amount of radish or cucumber.

Ground beef or turkey can be used instead of ground pork.

Cooking and Serving Tips: Fish sauce is very salty. Read labels and choose the one with the least sodium. Strain the lime juice for a clear sauce. Large, shallow bowls are the most attractive way to serve this salad. This recipe nicely fills six 7-inch bowls.

**Nutrition Facts**

- Calories 458
- Total Fat 20g 26%
- Saturated Fat 4g 20%
- Cholesterol 34mg 11%
- Sodium 529mg 23%
- Total Carbohydrate 53g 19%
- Dietary Fiber 4g 14%
- Total Sugars 9g
- Includes 6g
- Added Sugars 12%
- Protein 20g

## 5

# PULLED CHICKEN AND SUMMER SQUASH CASSEROLE

- Total Time: 75 min
- Prep Time: 45 min
- Cook Time: 30 min
- Servings: 8 (1 cup each)

Anaheim peppers are mild, yet flavorful, often used for chile relleno. They add just the right touch to this hearty main dish, which is perfect for enjoying the late summer bounty of your squash garden or farmer's market. If they aren't available, substitute poblano peppers. Serve this casserole with a green salad on the side.

## Ingredients

- 3 small summer squashes (total 1 ½ pounds)
- 3 fresh Anaheim peppers, seeded and chopped
- 1 ¾ pounds boneless, skinless chicken breast
- 1 teaspoon salt, divided
- 2 cups lactose-free milk
- 3 tablespoons cornstarch
- 1 teaspoon ground ancho chile
- ½ teaspoon freshly ground black pepper
- 6 six-inch uncooked corn tortillas
- 2 cups shredded Cheddar cheese, divided
- ½ cup cherry tomatoes, halved
- ¾ teaspoon crushed red pepper flakes (optional)

## Preparation

Preheat the oven to 400F. Lightly grease a baking tray and a 9x10-inch baking dish.

Slice squashes into 1/2-inch pieces and distribute in a single layer on the baking tray. Add the chopped pepper and roast until the squash appears about half done, 15 to 20 minutes. Remove the vegetables from the oven and set aside.

Reduce the heat to 350F.

While the squash roasts, slice the chicken breasts lengthwise. Place the chicken in the bottom of a medium saucepan or Dutch oven. Add just enough water to cover the chicken and season the water with 1/4 teaspoon of salt. Bring the pot to a simmer over medium heat; do not allow it to boil. Reduce the heat to low and simmer, covered, until the thickest part of the chicken breasts cook through, about 20 minutes. Remove the chicken to a plate and allow it to cool. Pour 1/2 cup of the broth into a heatproof measuring cup; reserve the rest for another use or discard.

While the chicken cools, in the same saucepan, whisk together the milk, cornstarch, ground chile, 3/4 teaspoon salt, and black pepper. Stir in the 1/2 cup of warm chicken broth and stir the mixture over medium heat until it thickens and begins to bubble, about 5 minutes.

Remove the white sauce from the heat. Spoon 1/2 cup sauce into the baking dish and top with 3 corn tortillas, tearing the tortillas as needed to arrange them in a single layer.

Use two forks to shred the chicken, then stir it into the sauce along with the cooked squash and peppers, 1½ cups of cheese, and chile flakes if using. Spread half of the mixture in the baking dish, top with three corn tortillas, then with the other half of the chicken mixture. Top with halved cherry tomatoes and sprinkle with the remaining 1/2 cup of cheese.

Bake until the sauce bubbles and the casserole is golden brown on top, about 30 minutes. Serve promptly.

Ingredient Variations and Substitutions: The meat from one pre-cooked rotisserie chicken can be substituted for the chicken in this recipe. The chicken meat can be cubed with a knife instead of shredded, if preferred.

To make the recipe gluten-free, use gluten-free tortillas.

Zucchini can be substituted for some or all of the summer squash.

Cooking and Serving Tips: Poaching the chicken over very low heat, as described, is the key to keeping it tender and moist. Boiling will toughen it.

This entree can be assembled ahead of time, refrigerated, and baked for about 40 minutes just before mealtime.

**Nutrition Facts**

- Calories 330
- Total Fat 14g 18%
- Saturated Fat 7g 35%
- Cholesterol 90mg 30%
- Sodium 570mg 25%
- Total Carbohydrate 20g 7%
- Dietary Fiber 2g 7%
- Total Sugars 6g

- Includes 0g Added Sugars 0%
- Protein 31g

## 6

# EASY SUNDAY MORNING BAKED EGGS RECIPE

- Total Time: 20 min
- Prep Time: 5 min
- Cook Time: 15 min
- Servings: 2 (2 eggs each)

These buttery baked eggs are a real treat; they taste as lovely as they look. For a low-FODMAP breakfast, serve these with potatoes, sourdough toast, or grits, with a side of lactose-free yogurt and blueberries. Serve eggs at the table in the ramekins they were baked in.

**Ingredients**

- 1 tablespoon butter
- ¼ cup finely shredded red cabbage
- 5 cherry tomatoes, halved
- 6 fresh basil leaves
- 4 large eggs
- ¼ teaspoon freshly ground black pepper
- 1 tablespoon freshly grated Parmesan cheese

## Preparation

Preheat the oven to 400F.

Divide the butter into two ramekins. Place them in the oven until the butter is melted and sizzling, but not browned, 4 to 5 minutes.

Carefully remove the ramekins to a heat-proof surface. Sprinkle the cabbage, tomatoes, and basil into them, and crack two eggs into each ramekin. Return to the oven and bake the eggs to the desired level of doneness, approximately 10 minutes.

Sprinkle with freshly ground black pepper and Parmesan cheese and serve promptly.

Ingredient Variations and Substitutions

Small amounts of other low-FODMAP vegetables can be substituted for the cabbage or tomatoes—shredded carrots, a handful of greens, string beans, or bell peppers, for example—but don't over-do it. Vegetables release moisture when they cook and too much might make the eggs watery.

Cheddar or gruyere cheese can be used in place of Parmesan.

Half a teaspoon of dried basil can be substituted for fresh basil.

Cooking and Serving Tips

If your ramekins are deeper and smaller in diameter, bake them at 350F for 17 to 18 minutes or until the desired level of doneness. For very small (1/2 cup capacity) ramekins, bake just one egg in each of four ramekins.

## Nutrition Facts

- Calories 220

- Total Fat 16g 21%
- Saturated Fat 7g 35%
- Cholesterol 390mg 130%
- Sodium 240mg 10%
- Total Carbohydrate 4g 1%
- Dietary Fiber 1g 4%
- Total Sugars 2g
- Includes 0g Added Sugars 0%
- Protein 14g

# 7

# TUNA FISH SALAD WITH FENNEL AND ORANGE SALSA RECIPE

- Total Time: 38 min
- Prep Time: 30 min
- Cook Time: 8 min
- Servings: 4

Fennel root, also known as anise, is a great stand-in for onion (a high-FODMAP ingredient) texture-wise. Like onions, it has an earthy root flavor—but with a licorice flavor all its own. Roasting mellows that flavor and also sweetens the taste. This delicious orange-fennel salsa serves as the dressing for seared tuna served on a bed of baby spinach.

**Ingredients**

- 2 teaspoons garlic-infused olive oil
- 1 teaspoon smoked paprika
- 1 teaspoon ground coriander
- ¼ teaspoon salt
- 1/8 teaspoon freshly ground black pepper
- 1 ¼ pounds fresh tuna steak
- 1 teaspoon canola oil
- 6 cups packed fresh baby spinach
- 8-ounce fennel bulb (1 bulb)
- 2 tablespoons plus 2 teaspoons garlic-infused olive oil, divided
- 2 medium oranges
- 5 Kalamata olives, pitted and finely chopped
- 2 tablespoons chopped fresh parsley
- ½ teaspoon dried oregano leaf
- 2 tablespoons cider vinegar
- ¼ cup thinly sliced scallion greens
- 1/16 teaspoon salt
- 1/16 teaspoon freshly ground black pepper

**Preparation**

Preheat oven to 425F. Spray a baking pan with baking spray or lightly coat with oil.

In a small bowl combine 2 teaspoons garlic-infused oil, smoked paprika, coriander, salt, and pepper. Brush tuna steaks on both sides with spice mixture and set aside.

Cut stalks off fennel bulb and discard. Cut the bulb in half through the root end. Cut out V-shaped "core" from each half at the root end and discard. Slice fennel halves into ¼ inch thick planks and place on the baking sheet in a single layer. Drizzle with 2 teaspoons of garlic infused oil. Roast until the fennel turns medium golden brown with some dark brown spots, 11 to 13 minutes. Turn the pieces over and roast until browned on the other side, 5 to 6 minutes. Remove from the oven and cool.

While the fennel is roasting, thoroughly wash one orange and zest it into a medium serving bowl. Squeeze the fruit to make ¼ cup orange juice. Peel and chop the fruit of another orange.

To the orange zest, add the juice, chopped orange sections, olives, parsley, oregano, cider vinegar, scallions, remaining 2 tablespoons of garlic-infused oil, salt, and pepper. Coarsely chop the cooled, roasted fennel and stir it into the orange salsa. Stir occasionally as the flavors blend.

Preheat a heavy skillet over medium heat; drizzle with canola oil. Add the tuna steaks to the pan and cook until browned on the bottom, 3 to 5 minutes. Turn and cook for 3 to 4 minutes on the other side.

Remove the tuna from the heat when it is still slightly pink in the center; it will continue to cook as it rests. This cooking time is for 1-inch thick tuna steaks; if cooking thinner steaks, reduce the time. After 2 to 3 minutes rest, slice the tuna into strips.

For each serving, plate 1 ½ cup baby spinach, add ½ cup Roasted Fennel Orange Salsa, then top with ¼ of the seared tuna strips.

Ingredient Variations and Substitutions: Instead of roasting the fennel, use it raw. Trim the bulb and slice it into paper-thin slices. Skip slicing the tuna into strips; cut the tuna steaks into 4 portions before searing, and place the whole piece on top of the salsa. One pound of cooked chicken or pork tenderloin can be used in place of tuna.

Cooking and Serving Tips: A fine rasp grater (Microplane brand, for instance) makes quick work of zesting citrus and makes it easy to avoid the bitter white pith. Citrus zest gives a great low-FODMAP flavor kick to any dressing or salsa.

Each serving is 4 ounces of tuna with 2/3 cup salsa and 1 1/2 cups spinach.

**Nutrition Facts**

- Calories 361
- Total Fat 17g 22%
- Saturated Fat 2g 10%

- Cholesterol 54mg 18%
- Sodium 401mg 17%
- Total Carbohydrate 15g 5%
- Dietary Fiber 5g 18%
- Total Sugars 8g
- Includes 0g
- Added Sugars 0%
- Protein 37g

# 8

# HEALTHY FISH TACOS WITH SPICY SAUCE RECIPE

- Total Time: 35 min
- Prep Time: 30 min
- Cook Time: 5 min
- Servings: 4 (2 tacos each)

These colorful fish tacos are Mexican-restaurant-tasty. Sautéing, instead of deep frying, the fish keeps them healthy and simplifies the preparation as well.

While there are quite a few ingredients (all of them low-FODMAP) the recipe comes together quickly and the cooking time is minimal. The light and crunchy cabbage slaw can be a stand-alone recipe as a side dish for any meal.

## Ingredients

- 3 cups finely shredded red cabbage
- ½ cup thinly sliced scallion greens
- ¾ cup slivered radishes
- 2 tablespoons fresh lime juice
- 1 tablespoon garlic-infused olive oil
- 1/8 teaspoon salt
- ¼ teaspoon sugar
- ¼ cup chopped cilantro, optional
- 2 tablespoons ground ancho chile
- 2 teaspoons ground cumin
- 1 ¼ teaspoons smoked paprika
- ¼ teaspoon salt
- 2 tablespoons fresh lime juice
- 5 teaspoons garlic-infused olive oil, divided
- ¼ cup mayonnaise made with olive oil
- 3 tablespoons lactose-free milk or water
- 1 ¼ pounds cod or other firm white fish, boneless, skinless
- 10 6-inch uncooked corn tortillas

## Preparation
To make the Mexican slaw

1. In a medium bowl mix together the cabbage, scallions, radishes, lime juice, oil, salt, sugar, and cilantro (if using).
2. Let the slaw marinate, stirring periodically, for at least 15 to 20 minutes.

To make the spicy taco sauce

1. In a large bowl, combine the ancho chile powder, cumin, smoked paprika, salt, lime juice, and 1

tablespoon plus 1 teaspoon garlic infused oil and mix to form a spice paste.

2. Transfer 2 teaspoons of this spice paste from the large bowl to a small bowl. Add mayonnaise to the small bowl and stir until smooth.

3. Whisk milk into the mayonnaise until the mixture becomes a thick but pourable sauce, adding more milk if needed. Set aside.

To make the fish

1. Cut fish into ¾-inch slices. Add fish to the large bowl with the spice paste and stir to coat. Heat a large skillet over medium-high heat. Add the last teaspoon of garlic-infused oil to the skillet, tilting the pan to coat with oil.

2. Add fish pieces, scraping in any spices and liquid from the bowl and cook, stirring gently until fish is cooked through and flakes easily, 3 to 5 minutes.

To prepare the tortillas

1. Place tortillas on a microwave-safe plate. Use a second plate of the same size and place it upside down over tortillas to make a lid. Microwave tortillas on high power until hot, soft, and pliable, 1 to 1 ½ minutes.

2. Top each taco with 3 or 4 pieces of fish and 1/3 cup Mexican Slaw; drizzle with Spicy Taco Sauce. Serve with plenty of napkins.

Ingredient Variations and Substitutions

If you like plenty of heat, add 1/4 to 1/2 teaspoon cayenne pepper to the spice paste before adding oil and lime juice.

Time saver: use pre-packaged shredded cabbage or coleslaw mix from supermarket produce section.

Use crunchy corn tortilla or tostada shells if preferred, or warm soft tortillas on a lightly greased griddle.


Cooking and Serving Tips

This recipe assumes the use of a mildly spicy ancho chile powder. If yours is too hot, reduce the amount to achieve your preferred heat level.

The slaw can be made several hours in advance and held, tightly covered, in the refrigerator.

**Nutrition Facts**

- Calories 470
- Total Fat 19g 24%
- Saturated Fat 3g 15%
- Cholesterol 84mg 28%
- Sodium 511mg 22%
- Total Carbohydrate 38g 14%
- Dietary Fiber 3g 11%
- Total Sugars 5g
- Includes 0g
- Added Sugars 0%
- Protein 38g

# 9

## SWEET SPICED PORK KEBABS RECIPE

- Total Time: 22 min
- Prep Time: 10 min
- Cook Time: 12 min
- Servings: 6 (2 kebabs each)

Pork and apples are a classic combination, but apples are high in FODMAPs. This IBS-friendly variation uses grapes instead of apples to lend sweetness, for a festive and attractive main dish or appetizer. Kebabs can be assembled ahead of time and refrigerated until grill-time for convenience.

**Ingredients**

- 1 teaspoon ground cumin
- 1 teaspoon ground fenugreek seeds
- $\frac{1}{4}$ teaspoon ground allspice
- $\frac{1}{4}$ teaspoon ground cardamom
- $\frac{1}{4}$ teaspoon salt
- $\frac{1}{4}$ teaspoon freshly ground black pepper
- 1 pound pork loin chop
- $\frac{1}{2}$ cup packed fresh basil (24 large leaves)
- 24 large red globe grapes

## Preparation

Soak twelve 10-inch wooden skewers in water for at least 20 minutes, to prevent the wood from burning on the grill.

In a small bowl, combine cumin, fenugreek, allspice, cardamom, salt, and pepper and set aside.

Cut the pork into uniformly sized 3/4-inch cubes. Sprinkle the spice mixture onto the pork cubes and stir until well coated.

Start each kebab by sliding a cube of pork onto the skewer. Wrap a basil leaf around a grape and thread onto the skewer so that the leaf is pierced in two places and trapped in place. Continue threading, alternating with pork cubes, until each skewer has three pieces of pork and two basil-wrapped grapes, being careful to leave no gaps. Leave room on the ends of the skewer to handle the kebabs.

Preheat the gas grill (or, if using charcoal, allow coals to burn until they are covered with a thin layer of gray ash). Grill for 10 to 12 minutes, turning occasionally until pork is only slightly pink in the middle, or to your desired level of doneness.

Ingredient Variations and Substitutions

Red globe grapes work best in this recipe, as their size and firm skin will help them survive grilling without falling off the skewer, but other grapes may also be used.

Kebabs can also be broiled. Place an oven rack about 3 inches below the heating element at the top of your oven and preheat the broiler. Line a baking sheet with aluminum foil and spread out the kebabs on top of the foil. Broil, watching closely and turning several times, until pork has reached the desired level of doneness. Grapes may start to caramelize in places and will soften somewhat.

Cooking and Serving Tips

To dry basil leaves after washing them, pat them with paper towels or spin them dry in a salad spinner.

Serve these kebabs on their own as an appetizer, or over greens in a salad. Or, serve them over a grain of your choice to make them into a hearty meal.

Fenugreek seeds are not often encountered in Western cooking and may be hard to find outside of specialty shops. If you can get your hands on some, they will probably be whole, and you will have to grind them yourself. You may want to toast them first, in a dry skillet, for some extra flavor. If you can't track them down, don't worry; this recipe will be lovely without them, too.

**Nutrition Facts**

- Calories 178
- Total Fat 9g 12%
- Saturated Fat 3g 15%
- Cholesterol 47mg 16%
- Sodium 132mg 6%
- Total Carbohydrate 9g 3%
- Dietary Fiber 1g 4%
- Total Sugars 7g
- Includes 0g Added Sugars 0%
- Protein 16g

# 10

# SPINACH AND PESTO SALMON

- Total Time: 25 min
- Prep Time: 15 min
- Cook Time: 10 min
- Servings: 6 (4.5 ounces each)

Salmon is the second most popular fish in America, after canned tuna. And why not? It is both nutrient-rich and delicious. Paired here with our low-FODMAP spinach and basil pesto (no garlic and just the right amount of cheese included), your dinner guests will enjoy a colorful and fragrant festival for the senses. Serve on top of balsamic vinegar-drizzled brown or white rice. Leftovers can be gently re-warmed or enjoyed cold, in a salad with chopped cucumber and diced tomato.

**Ingredients**

- 3 tablespoons olive oil
- 2 tablespoons water
- 1/8 teaspoon salt
- 1 tablespoon pine nuts
- 2 cups packed spinach leaves
- ½ cup packed fresh basil
- ¼ cup grated Parmesan cheese
- 2 pounds salmon fillet
- ¼ cup crumbled feta cheese

**Preparation**

Measure the olive oil, water, salt, pine nuts, and parmesan into the bowl of a blender or food processor. Add the spinach and basil leaves while the machine is running and process the pesto until a coarse paste is formed.

Position the top rack of the oven about 6 inches below the broiler and preheat it with the oven door ajar. Line a baking sheet or broiling pan with foil for easy clean up.

Cut the fish into 6 pieces and place fillets flesh side up on the prepared baking tray. Broil for 6 minutes, then flip the salmon over and broil until the skin is visibly blistered, about 2 minutes.

Remove the pan from the oven and use a fork to gently lift the skin off the salmon. Check to make sure the salmon is almost done; pull the flakes apart gently on one of the fillets using two forks. If it is not yet opaque at least 75 percent through, continue to broil for another minute or two. If it is almost done, spread the pesto evenly on top of the salmon fillets, then sprinkle with feta cheese. Return to the broiler for 2 to 3 minutes, until pesto is bubbling and feta is softened. Serve promptly.

Ingredient Variations and Substitutions

Any ratio of spinach to basil can be used in this recipe, so use according to your flavor preference!

Cooking and Serving Tips

Cooking time for salmon can vary significantly depending on the variety of salmon and the thickness of the fillets. Adjust accordingly.

To save time, purchase pre-grated Parmesan cheese.

Be sure to use full-fat feta made of cow's or sheep's milk. Reduced-fat cheese will not become soft under the broiler.

Refrigerate any leftover pesto, tightly covered, to use later on top of your favorite gluten-free pasta or as a sandwich spread.

**Nutrition Facts**

- Calories 300
- Total Fat 17g 22%
- Saturated Fat 4g 20%
- Cholesterol 79mg 26%
- Sodium 293mg 13%
- Total Carbohydrate 1g 0%
- Dietary Fiber 0g 0%
- Total Sugars 0g
- Includes 0g Added Sugars 0%
- Protein 34g

# 11

# BAKED SALMON WITH ALMOND FLAXSEED CRUMBS

- Total Time: 40 min
- Prep Time: 15 min
- Cook Time: 25 min
- Servings: 5 (5 ounces each)

This recipe combines the crunch of nuts and flaxseed with the texture of tender salmon for a main dish with lots of anti-inflammatory omega-3 fatty acids. The bulbs of the scallions are a source of FODMAPs, so using only the scallion greens in this recipe keeps it IBS-friendly.

**Ingredients**

- 1/4 cup toasted whole almonds
- 2 tablespoons flaxseeds
- 1/4 cup low-FODMAP bread crumbs (see how-to below)
- 1/8 teaspoon salt
- 1/4 rounded teaspoon dried thyme leaves
- 1/8 teaspoon ground black pepper
- 1/4 cup finely minced scallions, green parts only
- 1 teaspoon lemon zest
- 1 1/2 pounds salmon fillet
- 1 teaspoon garlic-infused olive oil

**Preparation**

Preheat the oven to 425F. Line a baking sheet (with sides) with foil.

In a blender or food processor, process almonds and flaxseeds until a uniform, sandy texture is achieved. Transfer to a small bowl and stir in the bread crumbs, salt, thyme, pepper, scallions and lemon zest.

Place fish skin-side down on the baking dish. Brush fish with garlic-infused oil and lightly sprinkle with salt and pepper if desired. Spread the crumbs evenly over the fish, pressing to adhere.

Bake fish until it flakes easily and crumbs are golden brown, 18 to 25 minutes.

Ingredient Variations and Substitutions

For an extra crispy topping, coat crumbs with baking spray or a mist of oil. Hold oil spray 10 inches above the crumbs. Spray evenly with a sweeping motion until crumbs look wet, then bake.

To make this recipe gluten-free, use gluten-free bread crumbs.

Cooking and Serving Tips

To make homemade low-FODMAP breadcrumbs, use any low-FODMAP bread, such as white, whole wheat, or spelt sourdough bread, or low-FODMAP gluten-free bread. Four 1-ounce bread slices makes 2/3 cup breadcrumbs, more than enough for this recipe. Here's how to make them:

Preheat the oven to 325F.

Cut bread into 1/2-inch pieces. Bake in a single layer until medium golden brown and dry, 15 to 20 minutes, turning once during baking.

Pulse bread in a food processor or blender until crumbs are the desired texture. If the crumbs are still soft, return them to the oven and bake until completely dry, 5 to 10 minutes.

No food processor or blender? Add the cooled, toasted bread to a zip-top bag and close, leaving a tiny opening. Crush with a rolling pin or pan bottom.

Toasting nuts enhances their sweet, nutty taste. If you aren't able to purchase pre-toasted nuts, you can make them yourself. Oven-toast nuts at 350F in a single layer until light golden brown, 10 to 12 minutes for whole nuts. Stir halfway through toasting. Nuts continue to brown even after removing from the oven and can burn quickly, so watch them closely. To grind nuts in a blender, get the blades turning in the empty blender and drop nuts in through the top center of the lid a few at a time.

Citrus zest (lemon, lime, or orange) packs a flavor punch in low-FODMAP recipes. A modern, steel, fine rasp grater is a low-FODMAP kitchen essential. The sharp teeth zest a whole fruit quickly and make it possible to avoid the white pith. The grater can also be used for hard cheese or chocolate and makes a little go a long way.

### Nutrition Facts

- Calories 293
- Total Fat 15g 19%
- Saturated Fat 2g 10%
- Cholesterol 73mg 24%
- Sodium 281mg 12%
- Total Carbohydrate 7g 3%
- Dietary Fiber 2g 7%
- Total Sugars 1g
- Includes 0g Added Sugars 0%
- Protein 33g

# 12

# LOW-FODMAP GREEK SHRIMP WITH FETA AND OLIVES RECIPE

- Total Time: 40 min
- Prep Time: 20 min
- Cook Time: 20 min
- Servings: 6 (3/4 cup each)

This tasty, easy recipe is suitable for a weeknight if you keep a well-stocked freezer, refrigerator, and pantry. Low FODMAP grains or starches like pre-made polenta rolls, or grains like quick cooking brown rice, quinoa, millet, buckwheat, or pasta, make you dinner-ready with little effort. This recipe also works well with any mild white fish.

## Ingredients

- 1 tablespoon garlic-infused olive oil, plus 1 1/2 teaspoons (divided)
- 1/2 large red bell pepper, chopped
- 14.5 ounce can diced tomatoes, undrained
- 2 teaspoons dried oregano
- 1/2 teaspoon smoked paprika
- 1/4 teaspoon salt
- 1/4 teaspoon ground black pepper
- 1/2 teaspoon crushed red pepper flakes
- 1/3 cup water
- 1/2 cup thinly sliced scallion greens, divided
- 1 1/2 pound raw, peeled and deveined medium shrimp
- 8 Kalamata olives, pitted, coarsely chopped
- 3/4 cup crumbled feta cheese
- 2 tablespoons chopped fresh parsley

## Preparation

In a large skillet over medium-high heat, warm 1 1/2 teaspoons of the garlic-infused oil. Add the bell pepper and sauté until tender, about 3 minutes.

Add the tomatoes, oregano, paprika, salt, pepper, red pepper flakes, water, and 2/3 of the scallions. Simmer until the liquid has mostly evaporated and the sauce is thick, about 10 minutes.

Add the shrimp and olives. Stir occasionally until the shrimp are cooked through, 4 to 5 minutes. When fully cooked, the shrimp will curl into tighter spirals and will appear opaque rather than translucent.

Sprinkle the feta cheese evenly over the pan without stirring it in and allow it to melt for 1 minute. Remove the pan from the heat and drizzle the remaining 1 tablespoon of garlic-infused olive oil over the pan.

Garnish with chopped parsley and the remaining scallion greens; serve over rice, polenta, or a grain of your choice.

Ingredient Variations and Substitutions: Frozen shrimp can be used in this recipe as well. Place frozen shrimp in a bowl of hot tap water until they are thawed, or mostly thawed, before adding. However, the best quality shrimp have never been frozen, and do not contain added salt or sodium phosphates. The nutrients in this recipe were calculated for shrimp that have not been treated with these additives, which can add up to 400mg of sodium per serving!

Fresh tomatoes can be used in place of canned. Use 1 1/4 cup diced tomatoes and add an additional 1/3 cup of water.

You may use finely diced leek greens rather than scallions and reduce the amount to 1/3 cup and do not reserve any for the garnish.

For a more complete meal, add some vegetables when you add the shrimp. Try 1 medium diced zucchini or 1 1/2 cups green beans (cut in 1-inch pieces). Both are low in FODMAPs.

Cooking and Serving Tips: Pre-cooked polenta rolls are a great item to have on hand in your pantry since they're easy to serve as a base for a meal like this one. Slice the roll into rounds 1/4- or 1/2-inch thick, brush or spray both sides with oil, and pan fry, turning once so that both sides are golden brown.

Quick-cooking brown rice can also make for a quick accompaniment to this shrimp. Alternatively, make yourself some "instant" rice: cook a large batch of regular brown rice, and freeze one-meal portions flat in zip-top bags. To serve, remove from the bag, break into several pieces, sprinkle with water, cover, and microwave until hot.

**Nutrition Facts**

- Calories 209
- Total Fat 10g 13%
- Saturated Fat 4g 20%
- Cholesterol 205mg 68%
- Sodium 1235mg 54%
- Total Carbohydrate 6g 2%
- Dietary Fiber 2g 7%

- Total Sugars 3g
- Includes 0g Added Sugars 0%
- Protein 24g

## 13

# 6-INGREDIENT ALMOND CRUSTED TILAPIA

- Total Time: 25 min
- Prep Time: 5 min
- Cook Time: 20 min
- Servings: 2 (1 tilapia each)

Eating leaner proteins like fish is a great way to help lower your cholesterol. If you're not used to cooking seafood, it can be a little intimidating at first. Tilapia is a great place to start. It's a very mild, tender white fish that's very versatile and not at all "fishy."

This almond crusted tilapia is a very easy, healthy recipe that's perfect for weeknights. Just coat the fish with an almond "breading" and bake. Then pair it with a steamed vegetable and serving of whole grains, and dinner is served!

## Ingredients

- 1/4 cup raw almonds
- 1/4 cup whole wheat panko bread crumbs
- 1/4 teaspoon freshly cracked black pepper
- 1/4 teaspoon garlic powder
- 1 lemon
- 2 (6-ounce) tilapia filets
- Finely chopped parsley, for serving (optional)

## Preparation

Heat oven to 375F. Line a baking sheet with parchment or a silicone baking mat.

In a food processor, combine almonds, panko, pepper, and garlic powder.

Squeeze lemon over fish fillets and coat both sides with almond mixture. Place on prepared baking sheet.

Bake for 10 to 15 minutes (depending on the thickness of fish) and then place under the broiler for 3-5 minutes to crisp.

Remove from the oven and enjoy.

Ingredient Variations and Substitutions

If you don't have tilapia, other flaky white fish, such as cod, will work.

This recipe will also work well with pecans or walnuts. Most nuts offer heart-health benefits.

Cooking and Serving Tips

Can't find whole wheat bread crumbs? Make your own by toasting a slice of whole wheat bread until crispy, then grinding it in a food processor or blender to form crumbs.

Watch the fish carefully under the broiler so that it doesn't burn.

Serve tilapia with a side of green beans or other steamed vegetables for a *q*uick and easy meal.

## **Nutrition Facts**

- Calories 320
- Total Fat 13g 17%
- Saturated Fat 2g 10%
- Cholesterol 70mg 23%
- Sodium 168mg 7%
- Total Carbohydrate 16g 6%
- Dietary Fiber 3g 11%
- Total Sugars 2g
- Includes 1g
- Added Sugars 2%
- Protein 38g

## 14

# CHICKEN, BROCCOLI, AND RICE CASSEROLE RECIPE

- Total Time: 45 min
- Prep Time: 15 min
- Cook Time: 30 min
- Servings: 9 servings (1 cup each)

It's important to consume a variety of food from all of the food groups to stay healthy and get all of the essential nutrients your body needs. I recommend building meals that consist of at least a lean protein, a whole grain or starch, and a fruit or vegetable. These components are all important to provide you energy throughout the day and help control your blood pressure.

It's easy to visualize when you have separate portions of protein, grains, and vegetables, but it can be harder to tell if you're getting a good variety of foods in mixed dishes like casseroles. This cheesy chicken, broccoli, and wild rice casserole are loaded with vegetables, whole grains, lean protein, and dairy. It's an easy and delicious meal that has all of the food groups in one, and one that your family will love!

This recipe tastes like comfort food but it is filled with fiber-rich vegetables and whole grains. It's even easier to prepare with frozen broccoli, leftover chicken, and leftover wild rice.

**Ingredients**

- 12 ounces boneless, skinless chicken breast
- 1/4 teaspoon sea salt
- 3/4 teaspoon freshly cracked black pepper, divided
- 2 tablespoons olive oil, divided
- 1/2 medium yellow onion, diced
- 2 cloves garlic, minced
- 3 cups frozen broccoli florets
- 1 tablespoon whole wheat flour or all-purpose flour
- 1 1/2 cups skim milk
- 3/4 cups sharp cheddar cheese, freshly grated, divided
- 2 cups cooked whole grain wild rice blend
- Cooking spray
- 1/4 cup whole wheat panko breadcrumbs

**Preparation**

Heat oven to 350F. Cut chicken into 1/2-inch cubes. Season with salt and 1/4 teaspoon pepper.

In a large skillet, heat 1/2 tablespoon of the oil over medium heat. Add chicken and cook, stirring, until chicken is cooked through. Remove chicken to a large bowl.

In the same skillet, heat another 1/2 tablespoon of oil. Add garlic, onion, and broccoli. Cook, stirring until onion is soft and broccoli is bright green. Pour into bowl with chicken.

Turn heat to low and add the remaining tablespoon of oil to

the skillet. Sprinkle flour over oil and whisk to make a paste. Slowly add milk, whisking to combine. Stir in cheese and remaining 1/2 teaspoon of black pepper. Remove from heat.

Add rice to chicken and broccoli in the large bowl. Stir to combine. Gently stir in cheese sauce.

Spray a 9x9-inch baking dish with cooking spray. Spread rice mixture into baking dish. Sprinkle with remaining 1/4 cup of cheese and breadcrumbs.

Bake 15 to 20 minutes, or until cheese is melted and casserole is bubbly. Remove from the oven and serve hot

Ingredient Variations and Substitutions

If you can't find whole grain wild rice, use brown rice instead.

For a vegetarian option, leave out the chicken.

Add any vegetables you have, such as carrots, cauliflower, spinach, corn or bell peppers.

Cooking and Serving Tips

This casserole is great reheated for lunch. To reheat in the oven, cover with foil and bake at 350F until warmed through.

Serve with a salad for extra vegetables.

**Nutrition Facts**

- Calories 218
- Total Fat 8g 10%
- Saturated Fat 3g 15%
- Cholesterol 34mg 11%
- Sodium 189mg 8%
- Total Carbohydrate 22g 8%
- Dietary Fiber 3g 11%
- Total Sugars 4g
- Includes 0g Added Sugars 0%
- Protein 17g

## 15

# SAVORY SPINACH AND FETA OATMEAL BOWL

- Total Time: 15 min
- Prep Time: 5 min
- Cook Time: 10 min
- Servings: 1

Oatmeal is one of the most heart-healthy breakfast foods in the American diet. It's soluble fiber helps to improve digestion, control your blood pressure, and lower cholesterol while keeping you full all morning. It can also help you control your weight.1 Oatmeal is also a great vehicle for healthy and tasty toppings like fruit, nuts, and spices; however, it's not often enjoyed with savory toppings.

Savory oatmeal is a way to pack protein and veggies into your morning meal while keeping sugar in check. This spinach and feta oatmeal bowl has 19 grams of high-quality protein, 5 grams of fiber, and a full serving of vegetables. It's one way to start your morning if you aren't a fan of sweet breakfasts.

Since cheese is usually high in sodium, make sure to keep the portion at one tablespoon and to buy low-sodium broth to keep this bowl of oatmeal blood pressure-friendly.

**Ingredients**

- 1/2 cup rolled oats
- 1 cup low-sodium chicken or vegetable broth
- olive oil spray
- 2 cloves garlic, minced
- 1 cup baby spinach
- 1 large egg
- 1 tablespoon feta cheese crumbles
- freshly cracked black pepper, to taste

Preparation

In a small saucepan, bring stock or water to a boil. Add oats and turn heat to low. Cook, stirring occasionally, until oats have absorbed all of the liquid, about 5 minutes.

Meanwhile, in a small nonstick skillet, sauté garlic and spinach. Remove from pan and set aside.

Spray skillet with olive oil spray and fry egg to desired doneness.

Spoon oatmeal into a bowl. Stir in spinach and feta cheese. Top with fried egg and a generous crack of black pepper. Enjoy!

Ingredient Variations and Substitutions

You can substitute steel cut oats or quick-cooking oats depending on how much time you have. Adjust the amount of broth based on package directions. Just don't use instant oats, as they typically have added sodium.

Use any vegetables you have on hand, such as bell peppers, mushrooms, or onions.

Cooking and Serving Tips

Round out this meal with a serving of fruit or enjoy alongside a non-sweetened beverage, like hot green tea.

**Nutrition Facts**

- Calories 309
- Total Fat 11g 14%
- Saturated Fat 4g 20%
- Cholesterol 200mg 67%
- Sodium 409mg 18%
- Total Carbohydrate 34g 12%
- Dietary Fiber 5g 18%
- Total Sugars 1g
- Includes 0g Added Sugars 0%
- Protein 19g

# 16

# KALE AND LENTIL STUFFED SWEET POTATO

- Total Time: 55 min
- Prep Time: 10 min
- Cook Time: 45 min
- Servings: 2

Making your own lunch can help you save money and stay on track when it comes to eating healthy. You know exactly what goes into your food (more nutritious foods) and what stays out (sodium, extra preservatives, and saturated fat).

This stuffed sweet potato is a great lunch option that provides vegetables, plant protein, and plenty of fiber to fill you up without weighing you down. It's also full of vitamins A, C, and K. It has no added salt and uses just a little bit of heart-healthy olive oil, so you can feel good about your lunch. Vegetarian sources of protein like lentils, are also very budget friendly and available in bulk.

## Ingredients

- 2 small sweet potatoes
- 1/4 cup dried lentils
- 1/2 cup water
- 1 teaspoon olive oil
- 4 cloves garlic, minced
- 4 large kale leaves, sliced into ribbons
- 2 tablespoons plain nonfat Greek yogurt
- 2 tablespoons parsley, chopped
- black pepper to taste

### Preparation

Preheat oven to 400F.

Rinse sweet potatoes and pierce with a fork in a few places. Wrap each potato in foil and bake about 30 minutes, or until tender. Remove sweet potatoes from the oven and keep wrapped in foil until ready to serve.

Meanwhile, prepare the lentils. Add lentils and water to a small saucepan and bring to a boil. Cover, reduce heat to low, and simmer 15-20 minutes or until lentils have absorbed all of the water.

Heat oil in a small nonstick skillet over medium low heat. Add garlic and kale and cook, stirring gently, until kale is wilted, about 2 minutes. Add lentils and stir. Remove from heat.

Remove sweet potatoes from foil and cut in half lengthwise, going only about halfway deep with your knife so that you aren't cutting all the way through the potato. Gently squeeze the two ends to open up the sweet potatoes. Fill the centers with kale and lentil mixture. Top with yogurt, parsley, and freshly cracked black pepper.

Ingredient Variations and Substitutions

You can use regular potatoes if you don't like serving sweet potatoes. If you don't have kale, use any kind of dark leafy greens, such as spinach, swiss chard, or mustard greens. For an extra protein boost, brown 1 ounce of ground chicken or turkey to add to this potato. Leave off the yogurt to make this a vegan meal.

Cooking and Serving Tips

Cook a batch of sweet potatoes and a pot of lentils on Sunday to keep in the refrigerator so you can make this meal and others in a snap during the week. This delicious stuffed sweet potato is also something you can make ahead of time. Prep and assemble more than one at a time for multiple healthy work lunches. That way, you always have time to eat a healthy lunch. Over time, skipping the $8+ sandwich and chips at lunch will not only save your wallet, but it will also keep you healthy!

To add even more veggies, serve this potato with a side salad or a cup of vegetable soup.

**Nutrition Facts**

- Calories 237
- Total Fat 3g 4%
- Saturated Fat 0g 0%
- Cholesterol 0mg 0%
- Sodium 65mg 3%
- Total Carbohydrate 42g 15%
- Dietary Fiber 10g 36%
- Total Sugars 6g
- Includes 0g Added Sugars 0%
- Protein 13g

# 17

# HEALTHY BUTTERNUT SQUASH GRAIN BOWL

- Total Time: 45 min
- Prep Time: 15 min
- Cook Time: 30 min
- Servings: 2 (1 bowl each)

Bowls are trending in a big way and are easily customizable to fit your dietary needs. I love making grain bowls for lunch as a way to use up leftovers like cooked whole grains or roasted vegetables. This Butternut S*q*uash Grain Bowl is a delicious seasonal version made with winter s*q*uash, apples, and dried cranberries.

Grain bowls made with whole grains, vegetables, fruit, and

nuts are great for your blood pressure since they are full of fiber and heart-healthy fats, potassium, and magnesium. Substitute any whole grains or vegetables you have, or include leftover grilled chicken or beans for an extra protein boost.

## Ingredients

- 1 cup butternut squash cubes
- 1 teaspoon olive oil
- 1 teaspoon maple syrup
- 1/4 teaspoon cinnamon
- 1/4 teaspoon freshly cracked pepper
- Pinch salt
- 1/4 cup pecans
- 1 cup cooked wild rice
- 2 cups baby spinach or spring mix
- 1 small Honeycrisp apple
- 1/4 cup dried cranberries

### Preparation

Heat oven to 400F. Line a baking sheet with parchment or a silicone baking mat.

Toss butternut squash with oil, syrup, cinnamon, pepper, and salt. Spread evenly on the baking sheet and roast for 25 to 30 minutes, stirring occasionally.

Place pecans on a piece of foil or small baking sheet and toast at 400F for 5 to 10 minutes or until fragrant, watching carefully.

Assemble bowls. Divide rice between two bowls. Add greens, squash, apples, cranberries and toasted pecans.

Ingredient Variations and Substitutions

Switch out the rice for any grains that you like or have on hand. You can also switch out the fruit, roasted vegetables, or nuts for any that you have on hand or prefer. Just be sure you choose unsalted nuts to keep the sodium low.

Add cooked beans, eggs, chicken or other lean meat for more protein.

Cooking and Serving Tips

Bowls are easiest when you have cooked whole grains in your refrigerator or freezer, so try cooking a batch of wild rice, quinoa, or farro for the week to make things easier. Even budget-friendly ones like brown rice and oats are a good choice.

Add a drizzle of olive oil, balsamic vinegar, or your favorite vinaigrette for even more flavor.

## Nutrition Facts

- Calories 377
- Total Fat 12g 15%
- Saturated Fat 1g 5%
- Cholesterol 0mg 0%
- Sodium 110mg 5%
- Total Carbohydrate 65g 24%
- Dietary Fiber 8g 29%
- Total Sugars 21g
- Includes 10g
- Added Sugars 20%
- Protein 9g

# 18

# BEEF, BROWN RICE, AND MUSHROOM SOUP RECIPE

- Total Time: 130 min
- Prep Time: 10 min
- Cook Time: 120 min
- Servings: 6 (1¼ cups each)

This hearty soup is reminiscent of beef and barley soup, as short grain brown rice has a similar appearance and chewy texture to barley. The timing suggested for this recipe assures that each ingredient is perfectly cooked and tender when the soup is done!

Fresh button mushrooms are high in FODMAPs, but fortunately, canned mushrooms are not. As they rest in the canning

water during storage, the mannitol in the mushrooms soaks out
and it is discarded when you drain the mushrooms.

## Ingredients

- 1 tablespoon olive oil
- 1 fresh garlic clove, chopped in large pieces
- 1/2 cup finely chopped celery
- 1/2 pound carrots, chopped
- 1 3/4 pounds beef chuck
- 1-**q**uart reduced-sodium, low-FODMAP chicken broth
  or beef broth (no onions or garlic)
- 1 teaspoon fresh thyme
- 1/4 teaspoon smoked paprika
- 1/2 teaspoon freshly ground black pepper
- 2 tablespoons tomato paste
- 1/3 cup uncooked short grain brown rice
- 4 ounces drained canned sliced mushrooms (yield from
  a 7-ounce can)

### Preparation

In a 4-**q**uart stockpot or Dutch oven over medium heat, heat
the oil and garlic together until the garlic begins to brown.
Remove the garlic and discard. Add the celery and carrots and
stir-fry them until they are lightly brown. Using a slotted spoon,
remove the vegetables to a plate.

Add the whole piece of meat to the pot and brown it for about
5 minutes on each side. Remove the meat to a cutting board. Pour
the broth into the stock pot and scrape the bottom with a spatula
to deglaze it. Stir in the thyme leaves, paprika, pepper, and tomato
paste. Cut the meat into 3/4-inch cubes and return it to the pot,
along with any juices that have formed.

Cover the pot and cook at a very light simmer for about 40
minutes. Add the brown rice and continue to simmer for 20

minutes. Add the mushrooms and reserved vegetables along with their juices. Simmer 30 more minutes, then serve.

Ingredient Variations and Substitutions

Half a teaspoon dried thyme can be substituted for fresh thyme leaves.

Cooking and Serving Tips

Beef chuck meat is ideal for soups and stews; if you are unable to buy a nice thick chuck steak for this recipe, buy a chuck roast and ask the butcher to cut it into two thick slabs for you. Pre-cut "stew meat" can also be used, saving a step, but you won't know what cut of meat you are purchasing and it may not be as juicy and tender as chuck.

**Nutrition Facts**

- Calories 240
- Total Fat 6g 8%
- Saturated Fat 2g 10%
- Cholesterol 70mg 23%
- Sodium 470mg 20%
- Total Carbohydrate 15g 5%
- Dietary Fiber 3g 11%
- Total Sugars 3g
- Includes 0g
- Added Sugars 0%
- Protein 29g

# 19

# ROAST CHICKEN WITH HOMEMADE GRAVY RECIPE

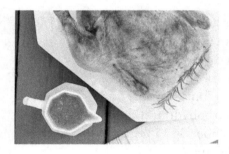

- Total Time: 135 min
- Prep Time: 15 min
- Cook Time: 120 min
- Servings: 10 (5 oz. chicken, 1.5 T gravy)

Roast chicken is a classic and a staple for people following low-FODMAP diets. This recipe is delicious enough for a small gathering at a holiday meal, yet easy enough to make weekly for a supply of fresh chicken.

Rather than add complexities to make this recipe "fancy," we've purposely kept it simple. Even if you have limited cooking skills and few kitchen tools, you can roast a chicken and make a low-FODMAP gravy. For newer cooks, it can be difficult to judge when a roast is done, so do purchase an inexpensive quick-read food thermometer and skip the guesswork.

## Ingredients

- 6 pound whole roasting chicken
- 1 teaspoon poultry seasoning
- 1 ½ tablespoons cornstarch
- 2 tablespoons cold water
- ¼ teaspoon salt
- ¼ teaspoon freshly ground black pepper

### Preparation

Preheat the oven to 450F. Brush or spray a 13 x 9 x 2-inch baking dish with oil.

Open the packaging around the chicken and drain the liquids into the sink. Place the unwrapped chicken breast-side-up in the roasting pan. Remove the package of giblets from the cavity of the chicken, unwrap, and place them in the roasting pan. Sprinkle the chicken with poultry seasoning.

Roast for 15 minutes, then reduce heat to 350F. Every 30 minutes or so, baste the chicken by spooning any accumulated juices over the top and sides of the bird. Start checking the internal temperature of the chicken after it has been roasting for a total of 1 ½ hours, then check again every 15 minutes until the temperature reaches 165F in the thickest parts of both breast and thigh meat. Total cooking time will be about 2 hours for a 6-pound chicken; if yours is larger or smaller, cooking time will vary. The internal temperature is more important than the timer for gauging when the chicken is done. Allow the meat to rest for about 10 minutes before carving and serving it.

While the chicken rests, pour the juices from the roasting pan into a measuring cup; fat rises to the top in just a few moments. If more than two tablespoons of fat are present, consider removing some of it, then add water, if necessary, to the 1 cup mark.

In a small saucepan, stir together the cornstarch and cold water, then whisk in the warm juices. Over medium heat, cook the gravy, stirring frequently, until it thickens and reaches a simmer. Stir in the salt and pepper and serve warm, with the chicken.

Ingredient Variations and Substitutions

Poultry seasoning may be omitted.

Cooking and Serving Tips

A quick-read food thermometer can be purchased for under 10 dollars at most grocery stores.

Do not rinse or dry the chicken before roasting it. Cooking the bird to 165F throughout will take care of any food safety concerns.

## Nutrition Facts

- Calories 320
- Total Fat 19g 24%
- Saturated Fat 5g 25%
- Cholesterol 105mg 35%
- Sodium 160mg 7%
- Total Carbohydrate 1g 0%
- Dietary Fiber 0g 0%
- Total Sugars 0g
- Includes 0g
- Added Sugars 0%
- Protein 34g

# 20

# LOW-CARB ASIAN CHOPPED SALAD RECIPE WITH GARLIC-GINGER CHICKEN

- Total Time: 35 min
- Prep Time: 20 min
- Cook Time: 15 min
- Servings: 4

Salads and satisfying usually don't go in the same sentence. But this Asian chopped salad is packed with protein from grilled garlic-ginger chicken, edamame, and tons of crunchy, raw vegetables. There's no shortage of flavor from bright, fresh herbs and a tangy soy-lime dressing.

## Ingredients

- 1 tablespoon sesame oil
- 3 cloves garlic (peeled and finely minced)
- 1 (1-inch) piece ginger (grated)
- 1/4 teaspoon salt
- 1 1/4 pound chicken breasts (boneless)
- 1 head butter lettuce (chopped)
- 1 (9-ounce) bag shredded cabbage
- 1 large carrot (peeled and grated)
- 1 cup edamame (shelled; defrosted if from frozen)
- 1 cucumber (chopped)
- 2 stalks celery (chopped)
- 2 scallions (chopped)
- 2 tablespoons mint (chopped)
- 2 tablespoons cilantro (chopped)
- 2 tablespoons soy sauce (reduced sodium)
- 1 tablespoon sesame oil
- 1 teaspoon honey
- Juice of 1 lime

## Preparation

In a small bowl, mix together sesame oil, garlic, ginger, and salt. Rub all over chicken breasts and place in a zip-top bag in the refrigerator to marinate for 8 hours.

When ready to cook, oil the grates of a grill and set on medium-high heat. When hot, place chicken on the grill and cook 5 to 7 minutes per side until grill-marked and chicken registers 160F in its thickest part. Remove from grill and set aside to cool.

While chicken is grilling, toss lettuce, cabbage, carrot, edamame, cucumber, celery, scallions, mint, and cilantro together in a large bowl. When chicken has cooled slightly, shred into bite sized pieces with a fork. Add to the bowl with the vegetables.

In a medium bowl, whisk together soy sauce, sesame oil, honey, and lime juice. Add to salad and toss to combine. Serve immediately.

Ingredient Variations and Substitutions

Don't eat meat? This salad can easily be made meatless by swapping chicken for tofu. Press the tofu dry, cut into bite-sized cubes, and toss with the ginger-garlic paste. You may want to add another tablespoon of sesame oil to help thin it down and coat the tofu. Skewer the tofu before grilling a couple minutes per side so it doesn't fall through the grates.

Although this salad is plenty filling, if you'd like to bulk it up a bit more with a complex carbohydrate, toss in a scoop of cooked brown rice or quinoa, both of which are packed with fiber and add to the protein count. You could also make it a noodle salad, mixing it with cooked and cooled brown rice noodles. Find them in the Asian aisle of most grocery stores.

Cooking and Serving Tips

Forgot to marinate your chicken? Don't worry—I always do that too! It'll still have plenty of flavor if you give it a quick 15 minute bath in garlic and ginger.

Stuck with leftover herbs after making this recipe? Blend the mint and cilantro together with olive oil and a bit of lime juice in a food processor for a tangy pesto to serve with fresh or roasted veggies. If you know you won't use up your ginger, peel it and store it in the freezer, where you can grate it from frozen using a microplane grater.

To save time, look for pre-chopped or shredded cabbage, lettuce, and carrots.

**Nutrition Facts**

- Calories 333
- Total Fat 13g 17%
- Saturated Fat 2g 10%
- Cholesterol 88mg 29%
- Sodium 552mg 24%
- Total Carbohydrate 16g 6%
- Dietary Fiber 6g 21%
- Total Sugars 6g
- Includes 0g

- Added Sugars 0%
- Protein 40g

# 21

# GLUTEN-FREE VEGETABLE, BEAN, AND CHEESE ENCHILADAS RECIPE

- Total Time: 35 min
- Prep Time: 20 min
- Cook Time: 15 min
- Servings: 4 (2 enchiladas each)

These gluten-free vegetable enchiladas with beans and cheese may give our family favorite Tuesday night tacos a run for the money. Not only are they easy to make, they're also a great way to use up any vegetables that are about to go bad—that's much better than tossing them!

Another thing that's great about these vegetable enchiladas is that they're packed with fiber from the beans, veggies, and corn, and they're also a great way to get your daily veggies in. In fact, some kids will happily gobble up kale when it's chopped into little, itty, bitty pieces.

## Ingredients

- 1 tablespoon avocado oil or vegetable oil, plus extra for greasing pan
- 1 medium onion, finely chopped
- 1 red, yellow, or orange bell pepper, finely chopped
- 2 cups tightly packed kale or other greens (i.e. spinach, chard, etc), finely chopped
- 2 cloves garlic, minced
- 1 cup frozen corn kernels
- 1 15-ounce can low sodium pinto or black beans, rinsed and drained
- 2 8-ounce packages enchilada sauce or 2 cups of your favorite homemade sauce, divided
- 8 corn tortillas
- 8 ounces grated cheddar or Mexican cheese blend, divided
- Optional, for serving: Chopped cilantro and green onions, sliced olives, plain Greek yogurt or sour cream, sliced avocado

## Preparation

Preheat oven to 350F. Grease a 13 x 9 baking dish with avocado/vegetable oil.

Prep the vegetables: Finely chop by hand or use a food processor with cutting blade attachment to chop onions, kale, and bell peppers (chop them all separately), then set aside.

Heat avocado/vegetable oil in a large skillet over medium heat. Add chopped onion and saute for 1 minute, then add minced garlic and saute for an additional minute. Next, add chopped pepper and saute for 1 minute, then add kale/greens and saute for 1 more minute. Add frozen corn kernels and beans, along with ½ cup enchilada sauce. Stir well to combine, and cook for 2 minutes, then remove from heat.

Wrap tortillas in a dish towel and heat in microwave for about 1 minute to soften, or heat individually in a skillet over medium heat. Spoon about ⅓ cup vegetable/bean mixture over a tortilla, repeating with remaining tortillas until all mixture is used up. Sprinkle 4 ounces of grated cheese, divided evenly, over tortillas and vegetable bean mixture. Carefully fold tortillas in thirds, and place each one seam side down in baking dish. Pour remaining enchilada sauce on top, and sprinkle remaining 4 ounces of cheese on top.

Bake in the oven for about 15 minutes, or until cheese is melted and bubbly. Remove from oven and allow to cool for 5 minutes before serving with (optional) cilantro, green onions, olives, Greek yogurt, and avocado.

Ingredient Variations and Substitutions

Black beans, or whatever beans you have in the pantry, would be equally delicious instead of the pinto beans. All are equally nutritious.

Have veggies to use up? These vegetable enchiladas are super versatile, and an easy way to use up any vegetables in your fridge or pantry that are wilted or need a little TLC. Some additional ideas include zucchini, carrots, tomatoes, cauliflower, eggplant, sweet potatoes, and so many more. Have fun being creative!

Cooking and Serving Tips

For serving, these vegetable enchiladas are a meal in themselves. Add some fresh fruit on the side and dinner is served!

Note: You can prepare the enchiladas ahead a day ahead, or in the morning, then keep them in the fridge, well covered, until you're ready to bake them.

**Nutrition Facts**

- Calories 543
- Total Fat 25g 32%

- Saturated Fat 11g 55%
- Cholesterol 54mg 18%
- Sodium 822mg 36%
- Total Carbohydrate 60g 22%
- Dietary Fiber 12g 43%
- Total Sugars 9g
- Includes 3g Added Sugars 6%
- Protein 25g

## 22

# CHICKEN CAESAR SALAD WITH HOMEMADE CREAMY CAESAR DRESSING RECIPE

- Total Time: 20 min
- Prep Time: 20 min
- Cook Time: 0 min
- Servings: 2

Many people order Caesar salads at restaurants in an attempt to eat healthy, but there are usually much healthier options when eating out. Between the cheese, croutons, and creamy dressing in most Caesar salads, saturated fat and sodium can quickly add up.

If you love Caesar salads, don't worry. You can still enjoy them at home and make them much healthier with a few simple changes. One of the easiest tweaks is to make your own healthy

Caesar dressing. This recipe is an easy dressing that uses protein-rich Greek yogurt for extra creaminess without added saturated fat. Garlic, dijon mustard, and a touch of parmesan cheese add lots of flavor without all the sodium you will typically find in most bottled dressings—and there are no anchovies.

Another way to reduce the sodium in your Caesar salad without sacrificing taste is to make your own croutons with whole wheat bread. Use a high-*q*uality parmesan cheese that you grate yourself so you get the most flavor out of just a little bit.

## Ingredients

- 4 cups Romaine lettuce (chopped)
- 1/4 cup onion (thinly sliced)
- 2 tablespoons parmesan cheese (freshly grated)
- 1 (8 ounce) grilled chicken breast (sliced)
- 1 slice whole wheat bread
- Olive oil spray
- pinch garlic powder
- 3 tablespoons nonfat plain Greek yogurt
- 2 cloves garlic
- 1 tablespoon dijon mustard
- 1 teaspoon Worcestershire sauce
- 3 tablespoon lemon juice
- 1/2 teaspoon fresh cracked black pepper
- 2 tablespoon parmesan cheese
- 3 tablespoon olive oil

## Preparation

To make croutons, preheat oven to 400 F and cut bread into cubes. Spray with olive oil and sprinkle with garlic powder. Spread into a single layer on a baking sheet lined with foil. Bake for 10 to 15 minutes, or until croutons are golden and crispy, stirring every few minutes.

To make the dressing, add all ingredients (yogurt through parmesan cheese) to a blender and blend until smooth. Slowly drizzle olive oil in while blending until you have a smooth consistency. Pour into a jar and store covered in the refrigerator until ready to use.

To make the salad, add romaine to a large bowl. Add sliced onion and parmesan. Pour in dressing and toss to coat. Sprinkle with croutons and divide onto 2 plates. Top with grilled chicken and serve immediately.

Ingredient Variations and Substitutions

This recipe can serve as a base for all of your Caesar salad needs. It's delicious as it is, but if you like a more elaborate salad, feel free to add more vegetables or top with nuts or chickpeas. You can also use another protein in place of the chicken, from shrimp or fish to steak, or even a vegetarian protein like tofu or beans. Get creative.

For gluten-free, use gluten-free bread. For vegetarian, leave out the chicken and use a vegetarian protein of your choice.

Cooking and Serving Tips

If you would like to pack this salad to take for lunch, leave the dressing off and mix it in when you're ready to eat.

**Nutrition Facts**

- Calories 363
- Total Fat 25g 32%
- Saturated Fat 5g 25%
- Cholesterol 55mg 18%
- Sodium 483mg 21%
- Total Carbohydrate 12g 4%
- Dietary Fiber 1g 4%
- Total Sugars 3g
- Includes 1g
- Added Sugars 2%
- Protein 23g

# 23

# GINGER ASPARAGUS CHICKEN STIR FRY RECIPE

- Total Time: 30 min
- Prep Time: 10 min
- Cook Time: 20 min
- Servings: 2 (2 cups each)

Boring, bland chicken and vegetables shouldn't be the first thing you think of when you're trying to eat healthily. Take them and add a hefty dose of flavor for a dinner that is both good for you and quick to make. All it takes is a few ingredients and a big skillet.

Ginger and garlic are two of my favorite spices for adding flavor to any dish. Skip the powder and go for the fresh versions—

it makes a huge difference! Plus, the combination of lean chicken, asparagus, and brown rice provides protein and fiber to keep you full and satisfied for hours. Just a touch of low sodium soy sauce adds a nice savory flavor without too much sodium, so you can keep your blood pressure in check.

**Ingredients**

- 1 tablespoon low sodium soy sauce
- 2 tablespoons rice vinegar
- 1/3 cup water
- 1 teaspoon sesame oil
- 1 tablespoon cornstarch
- 3 cloves garlic, minced
- 1 tablespoon ginger paste (or grated fresh ginger)
- 1 tablespoon lemon zest
- 1 tablespoon olive oil, divided
- 1 8 to 10-ounce boneless skinless chicken breast
- 1/2 medium onion, sliced
- 1 pound asparagus, cut into 1-inch pieces

For garnish: Chopped green onions and sesame seeds

**Preparation**

Whisk together all sauce ingredients. Set aside.

Cut chicken breast into 1-inch cubes and chop vegetables.

Heat half of the olive oil in a large skillet over medium heat. Cook onions in oil until soft, about 5 minutes. Remove from skillet.

Add remaining oil and turn heat to medium-high. Add chicken and cook, turning until all sides are browned, about 10 minutes. Add asparagus and cook, stirring, until asparagus is bright green.

Turn heat to medium-low and add onions and sauce. Cook, stirring, until sauce is thickened and onions are warmed through.

Divide between 2 plates and sprinkle with chopped green onions and sesame seeds (optional). Serve with cooked brown rice or quinoa.

Ingredient Variations and Substitutions

If you have other vegetables that you need to use up, such as carrots, mushrooms, or zucchini, add them.

You can use lean beef, pork, or shrimp in place of chicken if you'd like. Use low sodium tamari instead of soy sauce for gluten-free.

Cooking and Serving Tips

I like to buy the ginger paste in the produce section at the grocery store. It makes prep work so easy so that you can have dinner on the table that much faster.

Prep everything before you start cooking for the easiest cooking experience.

Serve with cooked brown rice or *q*uinoa to round out the meal.

**Nutrition Facts**

- Calories 255
- Total Fat 11g 14%
- Saturated Fat 2g 10%
- Cholesterol 48mg 16%
- Sodium 538mg 23%
- Total Carbohydrate 20g 7%
- Dietary Fiber 6g 21%
- Total Sugars 7g
- Includes 0g Added Sugars 0%
- Protein 21g

## 24

# HEALTHY BAKED CRAB CAKES RECIPE

- Total Time: 25 min
- Prep Time: 10 min
- Cook Time: 15 min
- Servings: 4 (2 cakes each)

Crab cakes are so reminiscent of summer. Full of delicious crab, they can transport you to a coastal vacation without ever leaving your house.

By making them at home instead of ordering them from a restaurant or buying them pre-made at the store, you can control everything that goes into them. That means tons of fresh lump crab meat, just enough bread crumbs to hold them together, and fresh vegetables and spices for flavor. You can also control what stays out of them—lots of sodium and fat.

These healthy crab cakes are lightened up by baking instead of frying, using just a bit of whole wheat bread crumbs and no added salt. It's all served with a delicious spicy Greek yogurt dipping sauce.


## Ingredients

- 1 egg plus 1 egg white
- 1 tablespoon dijon mustard
- Juice from 1 lemon
- 1/2 teaspoon paprika
- 1/4 teaspoon freshly cracked black pepper
- 8 ounces crab meat
- 1/2 cup whole wheat panko bread crumbs
- 2 cloves garlic, minced
- 1/2 jalapeno, minced
- 1 green onion, chopped
- Olive oil or oil spray
- 1/2 cup nonfat plain Greek yogurt
- 1 teaspoon dijon mustard
- 1 green onion, finely chopped
- Juice of 1/2 lemon
- 1/2 teaspoon cayenne
- Pinch freshly cracked black pepper

### Preparation

Gather the ingredients.

Heat oven to 400F.

In a large bowl, whisk together eggs, dijon, lemon juice, paprika, and black pepper. Stir in crab, garlic, jalapeno, and green onion. Gently stir in bread crumbs until just combined.

Form mixture into 8 patties and place on a baking sheet lined with parchment or a silicone baking mat. Lightly brush or spray the tops of each with olive oil.

Bake for 15 minutes or until the tops are lightly golden. Remove from the oven and serve with sauce.

To make the sauce, whisk together all ingredients from Greek yogurt through cracked black pepper, until smooth.

Ingredient Variations and Substitutions

Add more or less jalapeno and cayenne pepper based on your preferred spice level.

Cooking and Serving Tips

Make it easy on yourself by buying crab meat that has already been shelled. It should be near the seafood counter at the grocery store.

If you can't find whole wheat bread crumbs, make your own! Toast a slice of whole wheat bread until crispy, then blend in the food processor until large crumbs form.

Try these cakes over a green salad for lunch or share them with friends as a delicious summer appetizer.

**Nutrition Facts**

- Calories 101
- Total Fat 2g 3%
- Saturated Fat 1g 5%
- Cholesterol 102mg 34%
- Sodium 301mg 13%
- Total Carbohydrate 4g 1%
- Dietary Fiber 0g 0%
- Total Sugars 2g
- Includes 0g Added Sugars 0%
- Protein 17g

# 25

# NO SUGAR ADDED BLUEBERRY CRUNCH YOGURT BOWL

- Total Time: 3 min
- Prep Time: 3 min
- Cook Time: 0 min
- Servings: 1

Enjoying a serving of protein, fiber, and enriching antioxidants is a dietitian-approved way to start your day off strong. Even the most organized of us are sometimes short on time though, and all of us want something *q*uick but healthy to fill us up in the morning.

You'll only need a few minutes to put this recipe together. It's *q*uite versatile, so you can swap out the berries and seeds daily for a week's worth of variety. Plus, it's designed to offer more mono and polyunsaturated fats (the healthier fats) than saturated fat, making it a smart choice if you're looking to balance your cholesterol levels.

### Ingredients

- 1/2 cup blueberries
- 1/2 cup non-fat Greek Yogurt
- 2 tablespoons raw pumpkin seeds

### Preparation

Place blueberries in a microwave-safe bowl. Cover with a napkin and microwave for 45 seconds to one minute, watching closely to make sure the blueberries don't spill out.

Place Greek yogurt in a bowl. Top with the melted blueberries and pumpkin seeds.

Ingredient Variations and Substitutions

Both fresh and frozen blueberries will work for this recipe, or you can opt for another berry, like strawberries or blackberries. Similarly, swap out the pumpkin seeds for a heart-healthy nut like walnuts, almonds. Omega-3 rich chia seeds will also work, but might not provide the same satisfying crunch you're looking for.

If you're looking for something a bit more calorie-dense, double the recipe or increase one of the ingredients, such as the yogurt or pumpkin seeds.

Cooking and Serving Tips

The tastiest way to enjoy this 3-ingredient mixture is right after you take the blueberries out of the microwave. The hot, jammy berries contrast nicely with the cool, creamy yogurt. However, if you're really short on time in the morning, you can just as easily prep this the night before. Store it in the fridge in a mason jar for a grab-and-go morning go-to.

If you don't have a microwave, heat the berries over the stovetop, covered, with two tablespoons of water.

If you're using fresh blueberries, here's a tip: wash just the quantity you need, right before you use them, and store the rest in the fridge. If you store the batch washed, the excess moisture will decrease their shelf life.

## Nutrition Facts

- Calories 211
- Total Fat 9g 12%
- Saturated Fat 2g 10%
- Cholesterol 2mg 1%
- Sodium 60mg 3%
- Total Carbohydrate 18g 7%
- Dietary Fiber 3g 11%
- Total Sugars 13g
- Includes 0g Added Sugars 0%
- Protein 19g

# 26

# CHARRED WHITE BEAN BREAKFAST PIZZA

- Total Time: 10 min
- Prep Time: 5 min
- Cook Time: 5 min
- Servings: 1

This breakfast pizza is a good step towards a cholesterol-friendly diet. Between the whole wheat base, crunchy radishes, and creamy white beans, you get a whopping 12 grams of fiber (about 47 percent of your daily requirement) first thing in the morning.

Eating more fiber is one of the best diet tweaks you can make when working to lower your cholesterol. Why? It's been shown to help lower LDL levels (that's the "bad" cholesterol) and in turn protect your heart and lower risk of stroke, type 2 diabetes, and even obesity. As fiber travels through your digestive system, it binds with cholesterol molecules and helps carry them right out.

What does "eat more fiber" really mean though? You can read nutrition labels to choose foods that offer more of it and look up the grams of fiber in every whole food you eat. Or, you can take a simpler approach and aim to include more veggies, legumes, and unique whole grains in your meals (fiber is only found in plant-based foods!) to naturally increase your consumption—without overthinking it. A bit at every meal—even breakfast—adds up to help you meet your daily requirement.

## Ingredients

- 1/2 cup white beans
- 1 medium whole wheat pita, split in half
- 1/2 cup plain marinara sauce
- leaves from 4 sprigs fresh thyme
- 1/2 cup baby spinach leaves
- 2 large radishes, sliced
- 1/4 cup part-skim mozzarella cheese, shredded

## Preparation

Add white beans to a medium skillet and heat for 3 to 4 minutes, stirring a few times throughout. Remove and set aside when ready.

Split the whole wheat pita in half, so that you end up with two circles. Spread about 1/4 cup marinara sauce on each and place in the hot skillet, marinara sauce side up. Heat for 2 to 3 minutes then remove.

Sprinkle the thyme leaves evenly between the two halves, then the spinach, beans, and radishes. Sprinkle cheese on top.

Ingredient Variations and Substitutions: Regardless of the type of bean you use, you'll enjoy a good dose of soluble fiber (perfect for lowering cholesterol), filling protein, iron, and more.

Black beans and chickpeas, for example, would make tasty swaps. The same applies for the leafy greens. If you have kale on hand, opt for that instead, or try a few basil leaves instead of thyme for a more classic Italian taste.

Cooking and Serving Tips: To save time you can use canned white beans. Just be sure to rinse them before eating to reduce the sodium content. A simple rinse could decrease the sodium by up to 40 percent! What should you do with the rest of the beans in the can? Save them for lunch or dinner. Use them up in portable tuna pockets, for example, to continue with the veggie-forward theme for the day.

**Nutrition Facts**

- Calories 393
- Total Fat 9g 12%
- Saturated Fat 4g 20%
- Cholesterol 18mg 6%
- Sodium 1134mg 49%
- Total Carbohydrate 58g 21%
- Dietary Fiber 12g 43%
- Total Sugars 8g
- Includes 1g Added Sugars 2%
- Protein 23g

# 27

# TAKE-TO-WORK PORTABLE TUNA POCKETS

- Total Time: 20 min
- Prep Time: 20 min
- Cook Time: 0 min
- Servings: 1

Pita pockets are perfect for stuffing with healthy fare. In this recipe, you'll fill them with a unique tuna salad that offers two benefits over the traditional version—it's lower in fat because it swaps in creamy cannellini beans instead of excess mayo, and it's much higher in fiber because each portion is bulked up with veggies. These two benefits make it a fat-controlled lunch, perfect for those looking after their cholesterol levels.

**Ingredients**

- 1 5-ounce can water-packed chunk light tuna, drained and flaked
- 1/4 cup canned white beans, rinsed and lightly smashed with a fork
- 1/2 small red bell pepper, finely chopped
- 1 small stalk celery, finely chopped
- 1 small carrot, peeled and grated
- 1 small tomato, finely chopped
- 1/4 cup parsley, chopped
- 1/2 teaspoon salt
- 1/4 teaspoon cumin powder
- pinch turmeric powder
- 1 tablespoon low-fat mayonnaise
- 1 medium whole wheat pita, split in half and opened

**Preparation**

Combine all ingredients except the pita in a bowl.

Split the tuna salad between the two pita halves.

Ingredient Variations and Substitutions: This recipe can be used to "clean out your fridge." If you have leftover vegetables, chop them up and add them in addition to the ones called for, or just swap out the ones listed for whatever you have handy.

Shopping for white beans can be confusing! There are usually three types stocked on grocery store shelves: northern white beans, navy beans, and cannellini beans. Any of the three will work in this recipe.

Cooking and Serving Tips: Use whichever tomato you have available, but note that some may secrete more juices than others when you cut them up. Don't throw the juices away! Simply add to the mixture.

For a balanced lunch, enjoy both stuffed pita halves with a small side of soup, or have one with a larger soup portion.

## **Nutrition Facts**

- Calories 411
- Total Fat 8g 10%
- Saturated Fat 1g 5%
- Cholesterol 51mg 17%
- Sodium 1990mg 87%
- Total Carbohydrate 49g 18%
- Dietary Fiber 10g 36%
- Total Sugars 8g
- Includes 2g Added Sugars 4%
- Protein 39g

# 28

# SPINACH SPAGHETTI AGLIO E OLIO

- Total Time: 15 min
- Prep Time: 5 min
- Cook Time: 10 min
- Servings: 2 (1 cup each)

Jazz up this Italian-inspired pasta dish with spinach for a plethora of added vitamins and minerals. You'll get heart-health benefits from minerals like magnesium, important for a healthy heartbeat, and vitamins like folate, which may help reduce cardiovascular disease risk.1 The dark leafy green also offers compounds shown to protect your cells from damage and inflammation and it's an easy way to add some veggies to your meal.

This meal is one to make after a long day—it's not as time consuming, it's likely healthier and cheaper than take-out, and it offers a traditional comfort food aspect you're likely craving in the evening.

### Ingredients

- 4 ounces dry spaghetti
- 4 garlic cloves, sliced
- 1/2 cup parsley leaves, minced
- 1 tablespoon olive oil
- 1/2 cup spinach leaves, minced
- pinch red pepper flakes

### Preparation

Prepare and drain spaghetti according to package directions. Don't forget to salt your water and work on preparing the other ingredients while the spaghetti is on the stove.

Heat the olive oil in a medium skillet over medium heat. Add the garlic and red pepper flakes and sautee for about 2 minutes.

Add the cooked and drained spaghetti to the skillet and mix until incorporated with the oil and garlic.

Add the parsley and spinach, stir until well combined. Let cook for another 2 minutes before turning off the heat and plating.

Ingredient Variations and Substitutions: You can use a different type of pasta—fettuccine, linguine, even macaroni or penne—in equal amounts (4 ounces). A different dark leafy green such as kale, collards, or Swiss chard will work as well.

Cooking and Serving Tips: This is a perfect side dish for freshly made grilled chicken or salmon (if you have the time). Leftovers work, too.

You can also enjoy the dish on its own. Despite being a simple meal, you can enhance the presentation to make it more enjoyable. Use a nice plate, garnish with additional parsley leaves, and practice mindful eating while you enjoy every bite.

**Nutrition Facts**

- Calories 290
- Total Fat 8g 10%
- Saturated Fat 1g 5%
- Cholesterol 0mg 0%
- Sodium 41mg 2%
- Total Carbohydrate 45g 16%
- Dietary Fiber 4g 14%
- Total Sugars 1g
- Includes 0g Added Sugars 0%
- Protein 10g

# 29

# STICKY BAKED TOFU NOODLE BOWL RECIPE

- Total Time: 75 min
- Prep Time: 40 min
- Cook Time: 35 min
- Servings: 4

Noodle bowls can be easily adapted to make use of any vegetables you have on hand. It's a must to have the vegetables for this recipe cleaned and cut well ahead of time, before beginning to cook. Firm and extra-firm tofu are low in FODMAPs because the fiber from the soybeans has been reduced during the tofu-making process. The tofu is then packaged in a water bath, and any remaining oligosaccharides likely soak out of it. Pressing out this water before marinating the tofu helps it absorb the sauce and improves browning.

### Ingredients

- 1/3 cup plus 2 tablespoons water (divided)
- 1 1/2 teaspoons cornstarch
- 1/4 cup soy sauce (reduced sodium)
- 3 tablespoons light brown sugar (packed)
- 2 teaspoons ginger root (minced and peeled fresh)
- 1 tablespoon mirin
- 1 tablespoon rice vinegar
- 1 14-ounce package tofu (extra firm)
- 8 ounces rice Pad Thai noodles (uncooked)
- 2 teaspoons canola oil
- 2 garlic cloves (fresh, slightly crushed)
- 1/4 pound green beans (fresh, trimmed and cut in 1-inch pieces)
- 1 cup shelled edamame (frozen)
- 1 large carrot (peeled and cut diagonally into 1/8-inch thick ovals)
- 1/2 medium red bell pepper (seeded and cut into 1 x 1 1/2 -inch pieces)
- 2 teaspoons sesame oil (toasted)
- 1/2 teaspoon crushed red pepper flakes (optional)

### Preparation

Preheat oven to 400 F. Spray a rimmed baking sheet generously with baking spray or coat with canola oil.

In a small bowl, mix 2 tablespoons of water and cornstarch; stir until smooth and set aside.

In a small saucepan, combine soy sauce, remaining 1/3 cup water, brown sugar, ginger, mirin, and rice vinegar. Bring to a boil over medium heat, stirring periodically. Boil for 2 minutes. Turn heat down to a simmer, re-mix the cornstarch and water, and drizzle the cornstarch mixture into the hot sauce, stirring constantly. Simmer until the mixture thickens, about 1 minute. Remove from heat and set aside.

Over a sink, place the palms of your hands flat on both sides of the tofu block and squeeze gently with even pressure, like squeezing a sponge, until it becomes more difficult to see water coming out. Cut tofu in half lengthwise, then crosswise into a total of 16 pieces about 1/3-inch thick.

Place tofu on the prepared baking sheet. Brush each piece with a thin layer of sauce on both sides. Bake until the bottom edges of the tofu have caramelized, 14 to 16 minutes. Turn the tofu pieces over and return to the oven to bake until the bottoms have browned or caramelized on the edges, 8 to 10 minutes more.

While tofu is baking, in a large, covered stockpot, bring about 4 quarts of water to a rolling boil over high heat. Add the noodles and return the water to a boil, stirring gently several times to separate the block of noodles into strands. Begin testing for done-ness after noodles have boiled about 2 minutes and continue testing at 1-minute intervals. When noodles are tender, pour them into a strainer and rinse with cool water.

In a wok or large skillet on medium-high heat, warm canola oil, swirling to coat the pan. When the oil is hot, add garlic, green beans, and edamame and stir-fry for 1 minute. Add carrots and bell pepper and stir-fry for 4 more minutes, or until vegetables just begin to become tender. Remove the garlic cloves and discard (this keeps the dish low-FODMAP).

Add the remaining soy sauce mixture to the wok, stir to coat vegetables, and cook about one more minute. Remove from heat and stir in sesame oil and crushed red pepper flakes, if using.

Divide noodles into 4 bowls. Top each bowl with ¼ of the vegetables and 4 pieces of tofu. Serve with extra soy sauce if desired.

Ingredient Variations and Substitutions: For a rice bowl, replace the noodles with 4 cups of cooked rice.

Substitute ¾ pound of chicken for the tofu. Instead of baking, dice the raw chicken and stir-fry it in 2 teaspoons of oil until it is fully cooked. Set it aside, and return it to the stir fry along with the sauce just before serving.

To make this recipe gluten-free, use gluten-free soy sauce.

Cooking and Serving Tips: For extra convenience, use grocery-store prepared fresh or frozen green beans, peppers, and carrots. Sauce can be prepared earlier in the day and refrigerated until it is needed.

**Nutrition Facts**

- Calories 478
- Total Fat 12g 15%
- Saturated Fat 1g 5%
- Cholesterol 0mg 0%
- Sodium 685mg 30%
- Total Carbohydrate 72g 26%
- Dietary Fiber 4g 14%
- Total Sugars 14g
- Includes 10g Added Sugars 20%
- Protein 19g

**30**

---

# SHEET PAN CHICKEN AND POTATOES WITH FRESH GREEK SALSA

- Total Time: 75 min
- Prep Time: 45 min
- Cook Time: 30 min
- Servings: 4

Sheet pan dinners are a favorite of mine, not only for their easy clean-up, but also because they're the perfect blank slate for creating last minute healthy meals based upon whatever ingredients you have on hand. If you enjoy Greek cuisine as much as I do, trust me—you'll love the Mediterranean inspired flavors in this dish!

Naturally gluten free potatoes pair together deliciously with the lemon, garlic, and oregano infused chicken, but feel free to omit them for a lower-carb meal, or add in some extra veggies like green beans, asparagus, or broccoli—the sky's the limit!

**Ingredients**

- 4 small boneless, skinless chicken breasts or 2 large chicken breasts cut in half (~4-6 ounces per person)
- $\frac{1}{4}$ cup extra virgin olive oil
- $\frac{1}{4}$ cup lemon juice
- 2 cloves garlic, minced
- 2 teaspoon dried oregano, divided
- $\frac{1}{4}$ teaspoon salt, or to taste
- $\frac{1}{8}$ teaspoon ground black pepper
- 1 pound small yellow or red potatoes, cut into bite-sized pieces
- 2 cups grape or cherry tomatoes, sliced in half or thirds
- $\frac{1}{2}$ cup crumbled feta cheese
- $\frac{1}{2}$ cup pitted and chopped kalamata olives

**Preparation**

Combine olive oil, lemon juice, minced garlic, 1 teaspoon oregano, salt, and pepper in a large ziplock bag. Place chicken breast pieces in bag with marinade, seal, and place in refrigerator for 30 minutes or longer.

Preheat oven to 350F, and line a baking sheet with aluminum foil.

Chop potatoes and place on baking sheet. Add chicken pieces to the sheet, and pour marinade over potatoes. Using clean hands, toss potatoes and chicken in marinade to coat well. Place chicken and potatoes in the oven, and bake for about 30 minutes or until potatoes are cooked and chicken is no longer pink inside.

While chicken and potatoes are cooking, make the Greek salsa by combining the sliced tomatoes, crumbled feta cheese, chopped olives, and remaining 1 teaspoon of oregano. Keep covered in refrigerator until ready to serve.

When chicken and potatoes are done, divide between 4 plates, and top with Greek salsa before serving.

Ingredient Variations and Substitutions: This gluten-free sheet pan chicken and potatoes are easily made low FODMAP by omitting the minced garlic and adding 1 teaspoon garlic oil to the marinade instead. Infused oils, such as garlic oil, don't contain the FODMAPs that the whole food does. Fresh oregano is delicious in place of the dried oregano. As a general rule of thumb, use 1 tablespoon fresh herbs in place of 1 teaspoon dried herbs.

Cooking and Serving Tips: To save time, the chicken can be marinated overnight or in the morning, and the salsa can be made ahead of time and stored in the refrigerator for up to 3 days.

## Nutrition Facts

- Calories 426
- Total Fat 22g 28%
- Saturated Fat 6g 30%
- Cholesterol 89mg 30%
- Sodium 821mg 36%
- Total Carbohydrate 29g 11%
- Dietary Fiber 4g 14%
- Total Sugars 2g
- Includes 0g Added Sugars 0%
- Protein 29g

# 31

# ZESTY GLUTEN-FREE CITRUS, KALE, AND QUINOA SALAD

- Total Time: 35 min
- Prep Time: 15 min
- Cook Time: 20 min
- Servings: 5 (1 1/2 cups each)

This zesty citrus kale and *q*uinoa salad is a hit at every party I've been invited to, and my friends have always loved it. Loaded with greens, nuts, and fresh citrus, it's a true "superfood" salad that you can enjoy year-round.

Not only is it a perfect make-ahead dish to bring to a potluck, it's also a family friendly vegetarian meal. My kids never complain when I make this, but if your own kids aren't into kale, try chopping it up very finely (the onions too!) and throw in a little extra feta cheese in for good measure.

## Ingredients

- ⅓ cup lemon juice
- ⅓ cup extra virgin olive oil
- 1 tablespoon maple syrup
- Salt and pepper to taste
- 1 cup *q*uinoa
- 2 cups water
- ½ cup sliced or slivered almonds
- 1 cup finely chopped red or sweet onion (~½ large onion or 1 small onion)
- 2 large oranges, peeled and chopped into ~¼ inch pieces
- 4 cups kale, lightly chopped
- 1 cup crumbled feta cheese

## Preparation

Make the dressing: Combine lemon juice, olive oil, and maple syrup in a small bowl or mason jar. Stir or shake well to combine. Season to taste with salt and pepper. Set aside or store in refrigerator until ready to use.

Cook the quinoa: Add *q*uinoa and water to a medium size saucepan. Heat on high until boiling, then reduce heat to low and simmer until all the water has evaporated—about 15 minutes. Fluff cooked *q*uinoa with a fork.

While quinoa is cooking, heat a small to medium pan over medium heat. Add almonds and stir for about 3 to 5 minutes, or until light golden brown in color. Remove almonds from pan and allow to cool in a small bowl.

Chop the onions, oranges, and kale and add them to a large

salad bowl. Then add cooked **q**uinoa, toasted almonds, and feta cheese. Stir all ingredients well.

Add ⅓ cup of the dressing to the **q**uinoa salad. Stir well to combine and add additional dressing to taste if desired. Serve immediately, or you can cover and store in the refrigerator for up to 3 days.

Ingredient Variations and Substitutions

Mostly all of the ingredients can be substituted based on your food preferences or what you have on hand. Try baby spinach or chopped swiss chard in place of the kale. Use chopped green onion (green part only) in place of the red/sweet onion for a delicious low-FODMAP version. Substitute almonds with pine nuts, chopped pecans, or macadamia nuts, as desired.

Cooking and Serving Tips

This salad is equally delicious served warm or cold. My family and I eat this for dinner, then I enjoy leftovers for lunch the next day—either served cold or lightly reheated in the microwave.

## Nutrition Facts

- Calories 513
- Total Fat 33g 42%
- Saturated Fat 8g 40%
- Cholesterol 27mg 9%
- Sodium 305mg 13%
- Total Carbohydrate 43g 16%
- Dietary Fiber 8g 29%
- Total Sugars 11g
- Includes 3g Added Sugars 6%
- Protein 16g

# 32

# MEDITERRANEAN JEWELED COUSCOUS AND CHICKPEA BOWL

- Total Time: 35 min
- Prep Time: 10 min
- Cook Time: 25 min
- Servings: 4

Although it looks more like rice, couscous is actually a crushed wheat product more similar in nutrition to whole wheat pasta. Because of its small size, it cooks very *q*uickly, making it a great whole grain option for busy evenings. It's also extremely versatile and goes well with the flavors of many foods.

This particular dish combines couscous with pomegranates, sun-dried tomatoes, and pistachios, each of which adds their own unique health benefit. Additional fiber from spinach, protein from chickpeas, and creaminess from the kefir-tahini sauce tie the whole dish together.

**Ingredients**

- 1 can (1 3/4 cups) chickpeas
- 1 tablespoon olive oil
- 1/2 teaspoon cumin
- 1/4 teaspoon salt
- 1/4 teaspoon paprika
- 1/4 teaspoon cinnamon
- 1 cup whole wheat couscous, dry
- 1 tablespoon butter
- 1/4 teaspoon salt
- 4 tablespoons tahini
- 1/4 cup plain low-fat kefir
- 1 tablespoon lemon juice
- 2 cloves garlic
- 1/4 teaspoon black pepper
- 4 cups baby spinach
- 1/2 cup sun-dried tomatoes
- 1/2 cup pomegranate arils
- 1/4 cup pistachios, shelled

**Preparation**

Preheat oven to 400F.

Drain and rinse chickpeas. Toss them with olive oil, cumin, salt, paprika, and cinnamon. Roast for 25 minutes at 400F, flipping halfway through.

Cook couscous according to package directions, adding butter and salt to the pot before boiling the water.

Blend sauce ingredients in a small blender. Add water one tablespoon at a time to thin to desired consistency (2 to 4 tablespoons). Set aside.

When the couscous is done cooking, mix in sun-dried tomatoes, pomegranates, and pistachios.

Assemble bowls with a bed of baby spinach, then couscous and chickpeas. Drizzle with kefir-tahini sauce.

Ingredient Variations and Substitutions

Plain Greek yogurt can also be used if you cannot find kefir, however, then you might need to add a little more water to thin it out.

Top with goat cheese and fresh parsley if desired.

Cooking and Serving Tips

Leftover couscous works well as a side dish to fish or chicken.

**Nutrition Facts**

- Calories 500
- Total Fat 21g 27%
- Saturated Fat 4g 20%
- Cholesterol 8mg 3%
- Sodium 521mg 23%
- Total Carbohydrate 67g 24%
- Dietary Fiber 16g 57%
- Total Sugars 10g
- Includes 0g Added Sugars 0%
- Protein 19g

## 33

## SIMPLE BLACK BEAN AND BARLEY VEGETARIAN BURRITOS

- Total Time: 55 min
- Prep Time: 10 min
- Cook Time: 45 min
- Servings: 6 (1 burrito each)

Put together a batch of these bean and barley burritos for a few days' worth of heart-healthy, grab-and-go vegetarian meals. Being prepared can help you get closer to a cholesterol-friendly diet. When you're prepared you're less likely to choose unhealthier fare or order something in. Instead, you'll enjoy a delicious meal with ingredients you're familiar with.

## Ingredients

- 1/2 cup barley, dry
- 1 tablespoon olive oil
- 1 small onion, chopped
- 1 teaspoon dry garlic
- pinch red pepper flakes
- 1/4 teaspoon cumin
- 1/4 teaspoon salt
- 3 tablespoons tomato paste
- 1 medium carrot, shredded
- 1 15-ounce can black beans
- 6 large whole wheat tortillas (9 or 10 inches across)
- avocado, salsa, shredded cheddar, or sour cream, for garnish and dipping, optional

### Preparation

Prepare barley according to package instructions.

While barley is cooking, heat up olive oil in a medium-sized pan over medium heat. Add onion, garlic, pepper flakes, cumin, salt, tomato paste, carrot, and black beans. Stir together and let heat for about 5 minutes. Remove from heat and mash the mixture slightly with a fork.

Once barley is ready, place each tortilla on a separate plate. Divide the barley and black bean mixture into six parts and arrange them towards the middle of each tortilla.

Wrap your burritos.

Fold the tortilla in half, then tuck one edge under the stuffing and pull it back along with the stuffing.

Fold in the left side of the tortilla towards the middle (about 2 inches in). Repeat with the right side.

Tightly roll the stuffing until you have a perfectly rolled burrito.

Ingredient Variations and Substitutions

Black beans are rich in soluble fiber, an important part of a cholesterol-lowering diet. Fiber helps reduce LDL cholesterol specifically, likely by binding molecules as they travel through your digestive tract. The benefits don't stop there, though. You also get protein, which helps you fill up and avoid becoming hungry soon after your meal. In this way, beans are helpful for weight control too.

These benefits apply to all legumes, so if you don't have black beans or prefer lentils, white beans, black-eyed peas, pinto, or any other luscious legumes, go ahead and use them.

Using a whole grain like hulled barley also adds some fiber to your meal. The specific type of fiber, beta-glucan, also happens to contain cancer-fighting characteristics. When buying, you might notice that both hulled barley (sometimes called dehulled) and pearl barley are offered. Hulled barley is minimally processed, meaning most of its outer layer, the bran, is intact. Hulled barley is thus a whole grain. This outer layer is mostly removed in pearled barley, but some may still be present.

Additionally, fiber in barley isn't concentrated in just the bran but distributed throughout each kernel, so pearled barley still offers some fiber. If you're short on time, pearled barley will cook quicker. Otherwise, why not go for the hulled variety (or a different whole grain altogether).

Cooking and Serving Tips

Since barley takes some time to cook, aim to have it on the stovetop before you begin anything else. Another trick is to soak it overnight. Drain and rinse before putting it on the stovetop.

Serve with store-bought or DIY classic guacamole, ruby red salsa, or a sprinkle of shredded cheddar and creamy sour cream on the side. Instead, you can add these options into each burrito before rolling it up. Note that these add-ins are not included in the nutrition facts for this recipe, so be mindful of portion sizes.

**Nutrition Facts**

- Calories 408
- Total Fat 10g 13%
- Saturated Fat 4g 20%
- Cholesterol 0mg 0%
- Sodium 616mg 27%
- Total Carbohydrate 68g 25%
- Dietary Fiber 16g 57%
- Total Sugars 4g
- Includes 0g
- Added Sugars 0%
- Protein 14g

# 34

# SPICY ORANGE CHICKEN THAT'S BETTER THAN TAKE-OUT

- Total Time: 25 min
- Prep Time: 10 min
- Cook Time: 15 min
- Servings: 2

Chinese takeout is notorious for being full of sodium. Between the sugar and sodium-laden sauces, breaded meat, egg rolls, and fried rice, a takeout meal can *q*uickly add up when it comes to saturated fat and salt. A better option is to make your own at home. It may seem intimidating at first, but it's actually pretty easy and doesn't require too many ingredients.

This recipe for spicy orange chicken uses fresh orange juice, garlic, ginger, and red pepper flakes for tons of flavor without added sugar or salt. The only sodium comes from a little bit of reduced-sodium soy sauce, which research shows can actually reduce the amount of sodium in dishes without affecting flavor. Searing the chicken instead of breading and frying it and adding plenty of carrots makes this dish even more virtuous.

Serve this dish with a side of cooked brown rice or quinoa and top with sliced green onions and red pepper flakes for a super-easy version of takeout that is much healthier. It all comes together in less than 30 minutes—perfect for weeknight dinner!

**Ingredients**

- 3/4 cup orange juice, freshly squeezed (from about 2 medium oranges)
- zest from 1/2 an orange
- 1 tablespoon low-sodium soy sauce
- 2 cloves garlic
- 2 teaspoons grated fresh ginger
- 2 teaspoons red pepper flakes
- 2 teaspoons cornstarch
- 1 teaspoon sesame oil
- 1 boneless skinless chicken breast (8 ounces), cut into 1-inch cubes
- 2 medium carrots, thinly sliced
- 1 cup cooked brown rice or quinoa
- 2 sliced green onion
- red pepper flakes, to taste

**Preparation**

In a medium bowl, whisk together sauce ingredients. Set aside.

Heat oil in a large nonstick skillet over medium heat. Add chicken, stirring occasionally so that all sides get browned. Once chicken has browned, add carrots and cook, stirring, until carrots are softened, about 5 minutes.

Pour in sauce and cook until sauce is thickened, 3 to 5 more minutes.

Spoon into bowls with rice or **q**uinoa and sprinkle with green onions and red pepper flakes.

Ingredient Variations and Substitutions

To bulk up this dish even more, add more veggies like broccoli, snow peas, or cabbage.

For a gluten-free version, use low-sodium tamari instead of soy sauce, or look for gluten-free soy sauce.

For a grain-free version, use low-sodium tamari instead of soy sauce or arrowroot (or tapioca) starch instead of cornstarch and serve with cauliflower "rice."

Cooking and Serving Tips: This dish comes together quickly, so make sure your ingredients are chopped and prepped ahead of time to make cooking go more smoothly.

Each serving is about 1 1/2 cups chicken over 1/2 cup quinoa.

**Nutrition Facts**

- Calories 400
- Total Fat 8g 10%
- Saturated Fat 2g 10%
- Cholesterol 70mg 23%
- Sodium 402mg 17%
- Total Carbohydrate 47g 17%
- Dietary Fiber 6g 21%
- Total Sugars 12g
- Includes 0g Added Sugars 0%
- Protein 34g

# 35

# WILD BLUEBERRY CHEESECAKE SMOOTHIE

- Total Time: 5 min
- Prep Time: 5 min
- Cook Time: 0 min
- Servings: 1

Smoothies are a great way to pack a lot of nutrition into a single meal, especially if you're on the go. They can also be loaded with sugary syrups and fat if you aren't careful when grabbing a smoothie away from home. For a nutritious smoothie you can feel good about, skip the shop and make this tasty version at home.

Frozen wild blueberries are extra sweet and pack a lot of flavor and antioxidants into this wild blueberry cheesecake smoothie. They also make this smoothie extra cold and frosty without having to use ice. Research suggests that daily blueberry consumption could lower blood pressure due to the production of nitric oxide.

The Greek yogurt and avocado duo lends a luxurious creamy texture and also contributes healthy fats, fiber, and plenty of protein to keep you fueled and full. Make this smoothie for a sweet breakfast treat, or split it in half for a healthy snack or dessert.

## Ingredients

- 1 cup wild blueberries, frozen
- 1/2 small avocado
- 3/4 cup nonfat plain Greek yogurt
- 1/2 cup skim milk
- 1 teaspoon vanilla
- 1 teaspoon honey
- 1/2 lemon, juiced

## Preparation

Add all ingredients to a high powered blender and blend until smooth. You may need to add more milk to your desired consistency.

Pour into a glass and enjoy.

Ingredient Variations and Substitutions

You can typically find wild blueberries in the freezer section of your grocery store. If you can't find them, you can substitute regular frozen blueberries, but they will not be as sweet.

This is a great smoothie recipe to disguise veggies, so add a handful of spinach if you want to get a little more vegetable power.

To make this smoothie dairy-free, use dairy-free yogurt, such as Silk, and unsweetened dairy-free milk of your choice.

Cooking and Serving Tips

This recipe makes a meal-sized smoothie. For a post-workout snack or a healthy dessert, divide into two servings.

## Nutrition Facts

- Calories 376
- Total Fat 11g 14%
- Saturated Fat 2g 10%
- Cholesterol 6mg 2%
- Sodium 145mg 6%
- Total Carbohydrate 46g 17%
- Dietary Fiber 9g 32%
- Total Sugars 34g
- Includes 5g
- Added Sugars 10%
- Protein 26g

## 36

# SWEET AND SPICY TOFU AND JALAPENO PAD THAI

- Total Time: 40 min
- Prep Time: 15 min
- Cook Time: 25 min
- Servings: 6 (1 cup each)

This simple, lightened up version of an Asian classic will blow your mind by igniting your senses with a hint of heat from jalapenos. Plus, it's a low-fat, vegetarian option with tofu as the main protein source. It also offers anti-inflammatory properties from whole garlic cloves, as well as healthy fats from crunchy peanuts on top of rice noodles. According to the MIND diet you should eat nuts most days—at least 5 times a week, partly because they are a rich source of vitamin E, a nutrient that protects the brain.

This dish is also a good base for adding a variety of vegetables. With the MIND diet focus on vegetables—with at least a daily serving showing benefits against cognitive decline—this vegetarian pad thai fits in beautifully on a brain-healthy menu. Toss in leafy greens to give it an extra-special boost!

**Ingredients**

- 1 tablespoon peanut oil
- 2 garlic cloves, minced
- 1 small jalapeno, seeds and membranes removed, minced
- 1/2 cup mushrooms, sliced
- 1 package tofu, drained and cut into cubes
- 1 package pad thai rice noodles
- 1/4 cup lime juice
- 1/4 cup low-sodium soy sauce
- 1 tablespoon honey
- pinch chipotle crushed red pepper
- 1/2 cup peanuts, coarsely chopped
- 1/2 cup carrots, shredded
- 2 tablespoons cilantro

**Preparation**

On the stovetop over medium-high heat, place a wok or deep saucepan and add oil, garlic, peppers, mushrooms, and tofu. Saute until tofu is browning and vegetables are softened.

Prepare noodles according to package instructions. Add cooked noodles to the wok or pan with the tofu and vegetable mixture.

In a small bowl, whisk together lime juice, soy sauce, honey, and crushed pepper. Pour over the tofu and vegetables. Mix together while still over the heat. Remove when thoroughly heated.

Divide noodle dish among six bowls. Top each with a sprinkle of peanuts, carrots, and cilantro, if desired.

Ingredient Variations and Substitutions

Instead of tofu, feel free to add chicken breast or ground turkey breast if you're not vegetarian.

Toss in the mixed leafy greens, snow peas, or broccoli to add a pop of green to the dish.

For a nut-free version, use grape seed oil to saute veggies and top with crunchy radish slices.

Cooking and Serving Tips

Serve this dish immediately, warm, with chopsticks. Save leftovers in the fridge for a couple of days. Add more dressing to leftovers after reheating, if it needs a flavor boost.

**Nutrition Facts**

- Calories 332
- Total Fat 8g 10%
- Saturated Fat 1g 5%
- Cholesterol 0mg 0%
- Sodium 431mg 19%
- Total Carbohydrate 55g 20%
- Dietary Fiber 3g 11%
- Total Sugars 4g
- Includes 3g Added Sugars 6%
- Protein 10g

# VEGETARIAN HUMMUS BREAKFAST BAGEL RECIPE

- Total Time: 10 min
- Prep Time: 5 min
- Cook Time: 5 min
- Servings: 1

Breakfast bagel sandwiches aren't exactly the most diabetes-friendly breakfast. This vegetable-packed recipe allows you to enjoy a satisfying bagel breakfast without the blood sugar spike. Choose a 100% whole grain bagel and keep it open-faced for a filling and fiber-rich start to your day.

**Ingredients**

- ½ 100% whole grain bagel
- Nonstick spray
- 1 egg
- 2 tablespoons hummus
- 6 slices cucumber
- 2 tablespoons sliced roasted red peppers
- ¼ cup arugula
- 1 tablespoon crumbled feta

**Preparation**

Toast bagel.

Beat egg in a small bowl. Cover skillet with nonstick spray and heat on medium. Add beaten egg and cook, stirring frequently, until cooked through.

Spread toasted bagel with hummus. Top with cucumber, roasted red peppers, and arugula. Top with scrambled egg and sprinkle with feta cheese. Season with salt and freshly cracked black pepper, if desired.

Ingredient Variations and Substitutions

It's best to look for a bagel labeled 100% whole grain or 100% whole wheat versus ones labeled wheat or whole wheat. This means all the flour used is whole grain, rather than whole grain or whole wheat, which often use a blend of refined and whole grain flour.

If you cannot eat gluten, there are many whole grain, gluten-free bagels on the market. Or, swap in a slice of whole grain, gluten-free toast.

With so many different flavors of hummus on the market, you may want to add a kick of extra flavor to this recipe using spicy hummus, lemon hummus, or roasted garlic hummus. You could even use guacamole or ripe avocado mashed with a bit of lemon juice.

If you can't do a bagel without cream cheese, consider reduced fat, which lowers the saturated fat content without affecting the taste too much. I love this breakfast bagel with chive or roasted vegetable cream cheese.

In the summer, swap the roasted red peppers for a thick slice of juicy, fresh heirloom tomato.

Cooking and Serving Tips

My trick for making extra soft and creamy scrambled eggs is to cook it over moderate heat while stirring constantly. I like my eggs a little soft, but you can cook them until well done if desired. Scrambled eggs are extra delicious with a pinch of dried dill or basil stirred in. If you prefer a runny yolk, fry your egg over moderate heat, covering it with a lid for just a moment before it's done to help the white set.

**Nutrition Facts**

- Calories 299
- Total Fat 11g 14%
- Saturated Fat 3g 15%
- Cholesterol 194mg 65%
- Sodium 463mg 20%
- Total Carbohydrate 36g 13%
- Dietary Fiber 4g 14%
- Total Sugars 6g
- Includes 3g
- Added Sugars 6%
- Protein 15g

## 38

# SPRING BAKED PASTA WITH LEMON RICOTTA

- Total Time: 60 min
- Prep Time: 30 min
- Cook Time: 30 min
- Servings: 6 (2 1/2 cups each)

Yes, you can still have pasta if you have diabetes. This comforting pasta casserole is made with fiber-rich whole grain pasta, which helps maintain healthy blood sugar levels. With sweet asparagus, bright basil, and dollops of lemon zest spiked ricotta, every bite tastes like spring.

IRMA LOPEZ

### Ingredients

- 12 ounces 100% whole wheat penne
- 2 tablespoons extra-virgin olive oil
- ½ yellow onion, peeled and chopped
- 3 garlic cloves, peeled and minced
- 1 28-ounce can low-sodium diced tomatoes
- ¾ teaspoon salt
- ¼ teaspoon freshly ground black pepper
- ½ cup chopped fresh basil
- 4 cups chopped fresh kale, thick stems removed
- 2 cups asparagus, woody ends snapped off, chopped into 1-inch pieces
- ½ cup grated parmesan cheese
- 1 ½ cups part-skim ricotta
- zest of 1 lemon plus 1 tablespoon juice

### Preparation

Preheat oven to 400 degrees.

Bring a large pot of water to a boil. Add pasta and cook until slightly underdone. Drain and place cooked pasta back in the pot and set aside until ready to use.

Next, make the sauce. Heat olive oil in a medium pot on medium-high heat. Add onions and garlic and saute until golden, about 5 to 7 minutes. Add tomatoes, salt, and pepper and simmer 15 minutes until thickened and flavors have melded. Stir in basil and turn off heat.

While sauce is cooking, steam the vegetables. Rinse the kale off in a colander and transfer to a large microwave safe bowl. Heat in the microwave for four minutes then add to the pot with cooked pasta. Place asparagus in the microwave with 1 teaspoon of water. Microwave for 3 minutes until crisp tender. Add to pot with cooked pasta and kale.

Pour tomato sauce into the pot with the cooked pasta and vegetables. Stir until well combined. Pour mixture into a large casserole dish.

Mix ricotta cheese with lemon zest and juice. Dollop over the top of the pasta. Top with parmesan cheese. Place in the oven and bake uncovered for 30 minutes until casserole is golden on the top and slightly crispy around the edges.

Ingredient Variations and Substitutions

Many people with diabetes are afraid to eat pasta, but pasta can absolutely fit within a diabetic diet, especially when you choose high fiber, whole grain pastas. Look for ones that say 100% whole wheat or 100% whole grain, which are your best bet for blood glucose control.

You could also use gluten-free pasta. Ones made from brown rice or quinoa are also whole grain and beneficial for blood sugar control. There's also lentil or bean flour pastas, which have the added bonus of being higher in protein. Just be sure not to overcook these gluten-free pastas, which have the tendency to get mushy when overdone.

For more protein, feel free to add a pound of lean ground beef, turkey, or chicken to the tomato sauce. Or, you could mix in leftover rotisserie chicken. To keep it vegetarian but up the protein content, add a can of drained chickpeas or white beans.

Cooking and Serving Tips

If trying to make this dish on a weeknight, there are many time-saving tricks you can employ. Use defrosted frozen asparagus and kale (or spinach), just be sure to squeeze the greens dry with a dishtowel to get rid of extra liquids before using.

You could also swap jarred tomato-basil sauce, just look for one that's lower in sugar. Don't worry about finding one with zero grams of sugar though, since tomatoes naturally contain a small amount, and a pinch is often added to counteract the acidic taste.

This is also a dish you can make ahead and freeze for later. Freeze the pasta in an oven-safe casserole dish. To bake from frozen, place it in a 375-degree oven and bake for about 60 minutes until cooked through and golden.

Serve this with a simple side salad or slaw tossed with your favorite bottled dressing, or a simple mixture of balsamic or red wine vinegar and olive oil seasoned with salt and pepper.

## **Nutrition Facts**

- Calories 344
- Total Fat 13g 17%
- Saturated Fat 5g 25%
- Cholesterol 25mg 8%
- Sodium 505mg 22%
- Total Carbohydrate 44g 16%
- Dietary Fiber 6g 21%
- Total Sugars 6g
- Includes 0g
- Added Sugars 0%
- Protein 19g

# 39

# A HEALTHY STROGANOFF RECIPE MADE WITH CHICKEN

- Total Time: 95 min
- Prep Time: 20 min
- Cook Time: 75 min
- Servings: 6 (1 cup each)

All stroganoffs have one thing in common: sour-cream gravy. Now that lactose-free sour cream is available in some markets, even people who must avoid lactose as part of a low-FODMAP diet can enjoy this old-fashioned, stovetop meal.

To keep it low FODMAP, be sure to use canned mushrooms,

which are lower in FODMAPs than fresh ones, and choose a reduced sodium chicken broth that does not contain onions or garlic. Progresso reduced-sodium chicken broth is one that fits the bill.

## Ingredients

- 6 tablespoons sifted sorghum flour
- ½ teaspoon salt
- ½ teaspoon freshly ground black pepper
- ½ teaspoon dried thyme leaves
- 1 ½ pound boneless, skinless chicken breast, sliced into 3/4-inch strips
- 2 tablespoons garlic-infused olive oil, divided
- 1 medium red bell pepper, seeded and chopped
- ¼ pound fennel bulb, chopped
- 4 ounces drained canned sliced mushrooms (yield from a 7-ounce can)
- 1 tablespoon Worcestershire sauce
- 2 cups reduced sodium chicken broth
- ½ cup lactose-free sour cream
- 1 teaspoon Dijon mustard

## Preparation

In a shallow dish, stir together the sorghum flour, salt, pepper, and thyme. Dredge the sliced chicken in the flour mixture.

In a large skillet with a tight-fitting lid, heat 1 tablespoon of the oil over medium heat until fragrant. Reserve 1/4 cup of the red pepper for a garnish and sauté the rest with the fennel for about five minutes. Transfer the sautéed vegetables to a medium bowl.

Measure the second tablespoon of oil into the middle of the skillet and roll the skillet to distribute it. Add the chicken to the skillet; reserving the extra flour from the dredging dish. Brown the chicken on both sides, about 15 minutes. Scrape the bottom of the skillet with the spatula as you turn the chicken, so you don't lose the crust.

Return the sautéed peppers and fennel to the pan. Add the mushrooms, Worcestershire sauce, and chicken broth. Cover the skillet, bring it up to a simmer, then adjust heat to simmer gently for 45 minutes. Add the extra flour mixture and simmer until the gravy is thickened, 2-3 minutes. Turn off the heat, stir in the sour cream and mustard, and serve immediately over rice, garnished with the extra chopped red pepper.

Variations and Substitutions

If you aren't able to find lactose-free sour cream, consider using regular, full-fat sour cream if you think you can handle a little lactose, and stick to just one serving of the recipe, which will have just 1 1/2 tablespoons of sour cream in it and probably less than 1 gram of lactose.

To make this recipe gluten-free, use a gluten-free brand of Worcestershire sauce.

Cooking and Serving Tips

The secret to tender chicken is keeping this stew cooking at a simmer, not a boil. Adjust the heat as needed during each step of cooking to prevent boiling, which will toughen the chicken.

If your budget permits, purchase your chicken as chicken tenders or cutlets, to save a step during the preparation of this recipe.

If you will be preparing brown rice to go with this meal, start it when you are about to begin sautéing the vegetables. If the rice finishes cooking a few minutes before the stroganoff is ready, simply turn the heat off, leave the pot covered, and fluff the rice just before serving.

**Nutrition Facts**

- Calories 239
- Total Fat 11g 14%
- Saturated Fat 3g 15%
- Cholesterol 72mg 24%
- Sodium 490mg 21%
- Total Carbohydrate 10g 4%
- Dietary Fiber 2g 7%

- Total Sugars 3g
- Includes 0g
- Added Sugars 0%
- Protein 26g

# 40

# BEEF AND LENTIL CHILI WITH CORNBREAD TOPPING

- Total Time: 70 min
- Prep Time: 25 min
- Cook Time: 45 min
- Servings: 8 (1 ¼ cups each)

This hearty chili proves that you don't have to go without your favorite dishes on a low-FODMAP diet. This chili is nothing but delicious; it isn't missing a thing.

Canned lentils are the star ingredient here because they're lower in FODMAPs than lentils you boil from scratch because some of the FODMAPs will have passed into the canning water and can be drained away.

### Ingredients

- 1 tablespoon garlic-infused olive oil
- ½ medium red bell pepper, seeded, diced
- 1 ½ pound extra-lean ground beef
- ½ cup thinly sliced scallion greens
- 1 tablespoon plus 2 teaspoons ground ancho chile
- 2 ½ teaspoons ground cumin
- ½ teaspoon dried oregano
- ¾ teaspoon salt
- ¼ teaspoon freshly ground black pepper
- 1 14.5-ounce can diced tomatoes, undrained
- 2 tablespoons tomato paste
- 7 ounces drained rinsed canned lentils (yield from a 15-ounce can)
- ¼ cup water
- ½ cup lactose-free sour cream (optional garnish)
- 6 small fresh radishes, sliced (optional garnish)
- 1 cup medium grind cornmeal
- ½ cup sifted sorghum flour
- 3 tablespoons sifted tapioca starch
- 2 tablespoons sugar
- 2 teaspoons baking powder
- ¼ teaspoon salt
- 1 large egg
- ¾ cup lactose-free skim milk
- ¼ cup canola oil
- 1 cup shredded Cheddar cheese

### Preparation

Preheat oven to 350F.

In an extra- large (12-inch) skillet, heat garlic-infused oil on the medium high heat. Add bell peppers and sauté until softened, 3 minutes. Move the peppers to the side of the pan and add the ground beef. Fry beef, crumbling and stirring until browned and no longer pink, about 4 minutes. Combine meat with red peppers and stir in scallions, ground chiles, cumin, oregano, salt, and pepper.

Add tomatoes and their juices, tomato paste, lentils, and water, and stir until tomato paste dissolves. Lower the heat and simmer for 15 minutes. If you won't be baking the cornbread in the skillet, carefully transfer chili to a greased 2 ½-quart baking dish.

While the chili is simmering, in a medium bowl combine cornmeal, sorghum flour, tapioca starch, sugar, baking powder, and salt. Add the egg, milk, and oil to the dry ingredients and mix until smooth. Stir in the cheddar cheese. The batter should be thick but slightly loose and almost pourable. If it's too thick, add additional milk 1-2 tablespoons at a time. Spoon dollops of batter evenly over the top of chili and spread with back of the spoon almost to the edges, leaving a small border; the batter will spread out as it cooks.

Bake until the cornbread is golden brown and a toothpick comes out clean when inserted in the center, 18-25 minutes. Remove skillet from the oven; don't forget, the handle will be hot! Allow the dish to cool for 5 minutes, then cut into 8 wedges; serve with a dollop of lactose-free sour cream and sliced radish.

Variations and Substitutions

Ground turkey can be used instead of ground beef.

In a hurry? Skip the cornbread topping and enjoy your chili with rice, quinoa, corn tortillas, or tortilla chips.

Cooking and Serving Tips

You will need a large 11 to 12-inch oven-proof skillet to take this recipe from the stovetop to the oven. If you don't have one, the chili can be made in a skillet and transferred to a 2 ½ to 3 ½ quart baking dish for baking the cornbread.

The type of cornmeal used affects the texture and cooking time of recipes. It is a good idea to use the exact type of cornmeal that the recipe calls for. For example, this recipe calls for medium grind cornmeal. If you use stoneground cornmeal, with coarser, bigger particles, you can expect that a longer cooking time will be needed.

Note that tapioca starch and tapioca flour are the same things.

## Nutrition Facts

- Calories 465
- Total Fat 25g 32%
- Saturated Fat 8g 40%
- Cholesterol 98mg 33%
- Sodium 652mg 28%
- Total Carbohydrate 34g 12%
- Dietary Fiber 5g 18%
- Total Sugars 8g
- Includes 3g Added Sugars 6%
- Protein 27g

# 41

# LOW-CARB AVOCADO TUNA SALAD CRISPS RECIPE

- Total Time: 10 min
- Prep Time: 10 min
- Cook Time: 0 min
- Servings: 2

Tuna salad is a fan favorite easy snack (or lunch) option, but the classic mayonnaise-laden version isn't always the most nutritious. By subbing mayonnaise for ripe and creamy avocado and adding chopped fresh cilantro, this tuna salad is rich and flavorful without being too heavy.

## Ingredients

- 4 ounces canned tuna in water, low sodium, drained
- 1/4 ripe avocado
- 1 teaspoon lemon juice
- 1 tablespoon diced red onion
- 1-2 teaspoon finely chopped cilantro
- Pinch red pepper flakes
- Fresh cilantro, optional, for garnish
- Hot sauce, optional, for garnish
- 4 brown rice cakes

## Preparation

In a small bowl, combine the tuna, avocado, lemon juice, red onion, chopped cilantro, and red pepper flakes. Mix with a fork until roughly combined.

Serve tuna salad atop brown rice cakes. Sprinkle with fresh cilantro and a few dashes of hot sauce for a kick.

Ingredient Variations and Substitutions

Finding the perfect avocado is notoriously tricky, especially when you need it ripe right away. A great substitute for fresh avocado is pre-made guacamole that you can purchase at any grocery store. Not only is it convenient, but by substituting prepared guacamole for the avocado, you won't be as tied to a meal plan if you don't want to make the tuna salad right when your avocado is perfectly ripe.

When purchasing pre-made guacamole, look for kinds made with whole ingredients—all guacamole really needs is avocado, lemon or lime juice, salt, and sometimes onion and peppers.

Canned salmon would work equally well in this recipe and salmon is also an excellent source of brain-boosting omega-3 fatty acids. As with tuna, choose varieties canned in water and either low sodium or without added salt. I also love to use sardines, which are a more sustainable, omega-3 rich fish. Try it—you might actually like it!

Cooking and Serving Tips

While brown rice cakes are a nice light base for this tuna salad, feel free to serve it atop whole grain crackers or toast, or even as a nutritious dip with crackers or raw vegetables.

If you serve this for a party appetizer, or simply want to add more veggies to your day, try serving the tuna salad in "cucumber cups," a super fun finger food. Peel one cucumber lengthwise but only peel off half the skin, using what I call the "clock" method.

Imagine you're looking down at the cucumber from one end —you'll begin by peeling the length of the cucumber at twelve o'clock, skip one o'clock, peel another strip at two o'clock, skip three o'clock, and continue all the way around. Leaving some skin on not only helps your cucumber cup hold up well, but the remaining skin provides better grip when picking it up to eat.

Due to oxidation, avocados are infamous for browning quickly after being cut. Since you're only using ¼ of an avocado (or half of a half) in this recipe, one unique trick will help the remaining quarter stay fresh—a water bath! Place avocado half cut side down in a shallow dish with water just to the edge of the skin and store in refrigerator up to 24 hours.

**Nutrition Facts**

- Calories 101
- Total Fat 3g 4%
- Saturated Fat 0g 0%
- Cholesterol 15mg 5%
- Sodium 31mg 1%
- Total Carbohydrate 9g 3%
- Dietary Fiber 3g 11%
- Total Sugars 0g
- Includes 0g Added Sugars 0%
- Protein 10g

# 42

# STAMPPOT SEARED SALMON, MASH, AND KALE RECIPE

- Total Time: 60 min
- Prep Time: 30 min
- Cook Time: 30 min
- Servings: 4

Our friends in Northern Europe have many variations of potatoes mashed with vegetables, often topped with sausage. In Holland, mashed potatoes and kale are the main ingredients of a dish called stamppot. This recipe has a New England twist, where salmon and potatoes are traditional partners and are traditionally served together on the Fourth of July.

## Ingredients

- 1 ½ pound potatoes, peeled, cut into 2-inch pieces (4 medium potatoes)
- ½ pound kale, finely chopped
- ½ cup finely chopped leek leaves
- 1 tablespoon garlic-infused olive oil
- 1 ¼ pound salmon fillet, quartered
- 1/8 teaspoon dried dill
- ½ cup lactose-free milk
- 2 tablespoons butter
- ¾ teaspoon salt
- 1/8 teaspoon ground white pepper
- 4 teaspoons balsamic vinegar, optional

## Preparation

In a large stockpot, cover the potatoes with water and bring them to a boil over high heat. Reduce the heat, cover the pot, and simmer the potatoes for about 10 minutes. Add the kale and leek leaves; continue to simmer until the potatoes are tender, about 10 more minutes, stirring twice toward the end. Even though the kale and leaks will not be underwater when they are first added to the pot, the steam from the potato water will cook them.

Meanwhile, heat the olive oil in a heavy skillet over medium-high heat until it is shimmering and fragrant. Sear the salmon pieces skin side up in the hot oil until a golden brown crust has formed. Turn the salmon just once. Scrape the bottom of the frying pan with the spatula as you turn the salmon, so you don't lose the crust. Continue cooking, skin side down, until the fish is opaque when flaked with a fork. Sprinkle the salmon with dried dill.

Pouring away from you to avoid the hot steam, drain the vegetables in a colander. Return vegetables to the pot and mash them together with the milk, butter, salt, and pepper. Divide the potato mixture into serving bowls. Separate the seared salmon from the skin and place atop the potatoes. Serve drizzled with balsamic vinegar if desired.

When serving, each serving is about 5 ounces salmon plus 1 cup mashed vegetables.

Variations and Substitutions

If you don't eat dairy, you can mash the potatoes with olive oil and unsweetened rice or almond milk instead of butter and milk.

Cooking and Serving Tips

To make this recipe a breeze, wash, peel, and chop all the vegetables before you start cooking anything. Leek greens can be sandy at times, so chop them first, then swish them around in a bowl of water to rinse all the sand off.

The salmon skin tends to stick to the skillet, which makes it easy to separate it from the cooked fillet. Just slide a spatula between the two and they will separate easily.

Use the leftover white parts of the leek to make a low-FODMAP leek-infused oil, or try re-growing your leek greens by propping them upright in a glass of water.

**Nutrition Facts**

- Calories 456
- Total Fat 17g 22%
- Saturated Fat 6g 30%
- Cholesterol 84mg 28%
- Sodium 632mg 27%
- Total Carbohydrate 41g 15%
- Dietary Fiber 4g 14%
- Total Sugars 5g
- Includes 0g Added Sugars 0%
- Protein 35g

## 43

# LOW-FODMAP FISH CHOWDER RECIPE

- Total Time: 45 min
- Prep Time: 15 min
- Cook Time: 30 min
- Servings: 8 (1 ½ cups each)

Every cook has a favorite fish chowder. This one is reminiscent of those often served in New England chowder houses, with a thickened base rather than just milk. Instead of flour as a thickener, this version uses potato flakes to reach a creamy consistency, with or without the cream. Heavy cream has very little lactose, so there is no need to seek out a lactose-free version for the small amount in this recipe, to keep it low in FODMAPs.

## Ingredients

- 1 tablespoon butter
- 3 ounces sliced Canadian bacon, finely diced
- ½ cup chopped celeriac
- 1 medium parsnip
- ½ cup finely chopped fennel bulb
- 1 cup uncooked potato flakes
- 1 cup clam juice or water
- 1 cup water
- 5 cups lactose-free whole milk
- 1 ¼ pound red potatoes with skin, cut into ¼ inch cubes
- 6 scallions, green part only, thinly sliced, divided
- 1 teaspoon dried thyme leaves
- 1 bay leaf
- 1 teaspoon salt
- ½ teaspoon freshly ground black pepper
- 1 ½ pound cod or other firm white fish, cut into 1/2-inch chunks
- ½ cup heavy cream (optional)

## Preparation

In a large Dutch oven or stockpot over medium-high heat, melt the butter. Add Canadian bacon, celery root, parsnip, and fennel; stir periodically until vegetables brown slightly, 4 to 5 minutes. Add the potato flakes, clam juice, and water and stir until potato flakes dissolve about 1 minute.

Stir in the milk, potatoes, ¾ of the scallion greens, thyme, bay leaf, salt, and pepper. Bring the pot to a low simmer (do not boil) and cook until potatoes are just slightly underdone about 12 minutes. Stir periodically to prevent vegetables from sticking to the bottom of the pot.

Add the fish and simmer until fish becomes opaque white and

flakes easily, 5 to 8 minutes. Add the cream and the remaining scallions; simmer 1 minute. Remove the bay leaf from the broth before serving.

Variations and Substitutions

Replace cod with any other mild white fish such as tilapia, haddock, or flounder.

Swap out Canadian bacon for 3 ounces diced bacon strips (about 3 pieces). In this case, omit the butter and sauté bacon before adding vegetables, until the fat renders about 1 minute. Then add the chopped vegetables and proceed with the recipe.

Replace scallions with ½ cup finely chopped leek leaves, adding all of them along with vegetables.

Cooking and Serving Tips

Celeriac is also known as celery root, in case that is what it is labeled as in the grocery store.

When purchasing potato flakes, read the label carefully to avoid a product with added garlic or onions, which are high in FODMAPs.

**Nutrition Facts**

- Calories 335
- Total Fat 13g 17%
- Saturated Fat 7g 35%
- Cholesterol 74mg 25%
- Sodium 589mg 26%
- Total Carbohydrate 32g 12%
- Dietary Fiber 3g 11%
- Total Sugars 10g
- Includes 0g Added Sugars 0%
- Protein 24g

# 44

## MISO MARINATED STEAK WITH BOK CHOY STIR-FRY RECIPE

- Total Time: 40 min
- Prep Time: 20 min
- Cook Time: 20 min
- Servings: 6

Flank steak is an attractive and relatively economical way to serve steak, since each portion includes a few strips of meat rather than a large piece. The flavorful marinade for the steak doubles in this recipe as a stir-fry sauce for the vegetables. This dish tastes great served over short grain white or brown rice, so plan accordingly.

## Ingredients

- 1 tablespoon minced, peeled fresh ginger root
- 3 tablespoons miso paste
- 2 tablespoons mirin
- 2 tablespoons reduced sodium soy sauce
- 3 tablespoons water
- 2 tablespoons rice vinegar
- 1 tablespoon plus 1 teaspoon sesame oil
- 2 teaspoons sugar
- 1 ½ pound flank steak
- 2 teaspoons canola oil
- 1 pound baby bok choy
- ½ large red bell pepper, cut in 1/2-inch pieces
- ¾ cup drained canned mushrooms (4 ounces dry weight)

## Preparation

In a small bowl, whisk together the ginger, miso, mirin, soy sauce, water, vinegar, sesame oil, and sugar until the sugar is dissolved and the mixture has a smooth texture. Remove ¼ cup of the miso marinade to a small bowl and set aside for the vegetable stir-fry.

Place the steak in a 1 gallon zip-top bag and pour in the remaining miso marinade. Seal the bag, removing as much as air as possible, and refrigerate the steak for 1 to 24 hours.

Grill the steak on both sides to the desired level of doneness, brushing several times with marinade from the bag. Remove the steak to a cutting board and cover it with foil to rest.

Slice baby bok choy lengthwise into halves. If baby bok choy is more than one inch in diameter, slice it lengthwise into quarters. Wash the bok choy, swishing vigorously and paying attention to the root end where sand can hide. Drain, rinse, and repeat.

Heat a large skillet over medium high heat. When wok is hot, add oil; then add bok choy and red pepper and stir-fry until char marks appear, 3 to 5 minutes. Stir in the mushrooms. Add the reserved ¼ cup of marinade and stir-fry until bok choy is tender, 1 to 3 minutes.

Just before serving, slice steak across the grain while holding the knife at a 45-degree angle into ¼ inch thick slices. Serve the vegetables and steak strips over cooked rice.

Variations and Substitutions

Substitute baby bok choy with a 1 pound head of regular bok choy prepared as follows: cut leaves off where they join white stalks and slice leaves crosswise into 1-inch thick strips, wash, and set aside. Cut end root off stalks and discard root. Cut stalks crosswise into ½ inch thick pieces. Stir fry stalks first with bell pepper until softened and charred in spots, 4 to 6 minutes. Add leaves and mushrooms together, stir fry 1 minute, then add reserved marinade and stir fry 1 minute more.

If you wish to turn the leftover marinade into extra sauce, boil it for one minutes in a separate small saucepan to cook it thoroughly before adding it to the vegetables in the skillet.

To make this recipe gluten-free, use gluten-free soy sauce or gluten-free tamari.

Cooking and Serving Tips

Canned mushrooms are not created e*q*ual. Avoid the cheapest brands; they are not nearly as tasty. The amount of mushrooms called for in this recipe, ¾ cup drained, is the yield from a 7-ounce can, which may also be described as "4 ounce dry weight" on the front of the package.

Assemble bowls or plates before serving, or serve family-style, passing a platter of beef strips, rice, and vegetables separately. One serving should be about 3 ounces steak plus 2/3 cup vegetables and salt.

**Nutrition Facts**

- Calories 305
- Total Fat 14g 18%
- Saturated Fat 4g 20%
- Cholesterol 90mg 30%

- Sodium 648mg 28%
- Total Carbohydrate 11g 4%
- Dietary Fiber 2g 7%
- Total Sugars 6g
- Includes 1g Added Sugars 2%
- Protein 35g

45

# TOMATO AND BROCCOLI BROILED TOP BREAKFAST FRITTATA

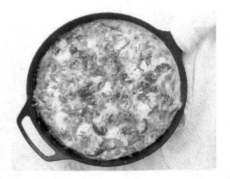

- Total Time: 25 min
- Prep Time: 15 min
- Cook Time: 10 min
- Servings: 4

If you're like me and a big fan of hitting the snooze button, then you know that making a nutritious and filling breakfast can be a challenge. Prepare this veggie packed frittata on the weekend and enjoy a slice for a grab-and-go breakfast. Your stomach will thank you!

## Ingredients

- 8 eggs, beaten
- ¼ teaspoon salt
- ¼ teaspoon freshly ground black pepper
- 1 tablespoon extra-virgin olive oil
- ½ yellow onion, peeled and chopped
- 1 large tomato, chopped
- 2 cups frozen broccoli florets, defrosted
- 1 ounce goat cheese

## Preparation

Beat eggs together with salt and pepper in a large bowl until well combined. Place rack in the middle of the oven and preheat broiler.

Heat olive oil in a large, ovenproof skillet on medium heat. Add onion and saute until translucent, about 3 minutes. Stir in tomato and cook until tender, about 2 minutes. Stir in broccoli.

Pour in beaten egg and move around until it covers the pan completely. Cook the frittata until it's starting to set around the edges, then sprinkle the top with goat cheese. Place the frittata under the broiler to cook through. It should only take a minute and keep a close eye on it to make sure it doesn't burn.

With an oven-mitted hand, remove from oven, let cool slightly, then invert onto a serving plate, Cut into four slices and serve or refrigerate until ready to eat.

Ingredient Variations and Substitutions

I love to make frittatas as an easy and satisfying breakfast throughout the year and switch things up based on what vegetables are in season. Try heirloom tomatoes, basil, and mozzarella in the summer, kale and cheddar in the fall, cauliflower and feta in the winter, and asparagus and goat cheese in the spring.

If you'd like to reduce the amount of cholesterol in this recipe, replace some of the whole eggs with egg whites. You'll need 2 whites for every egg being replaced. You could also replace 2 eggs with ½ cup milk or unsweetened, unflavored plant milk.

To make this dairy free, simply leave out the goat cheese.

If you like your eggs with hot sauce, stir a teaspoon into the beaten egg or douse generously with your favorite hot sauce to serve. I also like it topped with fresh herbs, like chives, green onions, or parsley.

Cooking and Serving Tips

Another fun option is to turn this recipe into mini-frittatas baked in a muffin tin. They're perfect for snacks or sandwiched between a whole grain English muffin or mini-bagel to make a breakfast sandwich. To make, crack an egg into 8 wells sprayed with oil, season with a bit of salt and pepper, then whisk together with a fork. Divide the sauteed onions, tomatoes, and defrosted broccoli between the wells then bake in a 350 degree oven for about 20 minutes.

To include a serving of healthy carbs with this meal, serve this with a slice or two of whole grain toast or English muffin, a side of fresh fruit, or add cubes or slices of steamed sweet or white potatoes to the frittata.

This frittata also makes a delicious dinner. Serve with whole grain bread or roasted potatoes and a side salad dressed with a quick dressing of equal parts lemon juice, olive oil, and a teaspoon of mustard to emulsify.

This frittata will last 5 days covered in the refrigerator. Serve warm, reheated in the microwave for 30 seconds, or at room temperature.

**Nutrition Facts**

- Calories 172
- Total Fat 12g 15%
- Saturated Fat 4g 20%
- Cholesterol 238mg 79%
- Sodium 273mg 12%
- Total Carbohydrate 6g 2%
- Dietary Fiber 2g 7%
- Total Sugars 3g

- Includes 0g Added Sugars 0%
- Protein 12g

## 46

# PEANUT BUTTER CUP CHIA PUDDING

- Total Time: 5 min
- Prep Time: 5 min
- Cook Time: 0 min
- Servings: 1

What if you could have a healthy breakfast that tasted like peanut butter cups? Good news—you can! You can turn nutritious ingredients like peanut butter, milk, and chia seeds into a tasty, easy to make meal that will keep you full and feeling good all morning!

Chia seeds are known as a "superfood" because they are full of fiber, protein, and healthy omega-3 fatty acids. They swell in liquid, making a 'pudding' that you can flavor with limitless healthy ingredients to fit your tastes. Of course, no single food can automatically make you healthy, but replacing a fiberless sugary cereal with chia pudding is a step toward healthier habits. You can make a serving or two ahead at night and it will be ready to eat in the morning.

The delicious combination of peanut butter and cocoa powder, along with skim milk and chia seeds, is one that is full of fiber, protein, antioxidants, and healthy fat that will keep you full and satisfied for hours while also keeping your blood pressure healthy.

## Ingredients

- 1/2 tablespoon unsweetened cocoa powder
- 1 tablespoon natural peanut butter
- 1 teaspoon honey (optional)
- 1 cup skim milk or milk of choice
- 3 tablespoons chia seeds
- For topping: additional peanut butter, mini chocolate chips or cacao nibs, or chopped unsalted peanuts

## Preparation

In a jar or other container with a lid, whisk together cocoa powder, peanut butter, honey (if using) and milk.

Stir in chia seeds. Refrigerate at least 6 hours or overnight.

In the morning, top with peanut butter, peanuts and/or mini chocolate chips and enjoy.

Ingredient Variations and Substitutions

Use almond butter or sunflower seed butter in place of peanut butter, if desired. The nutrition breakdowns for different nut butters are similar.

For vegan, use non-dairy milk of choice, agave, or maple syrup in place of honey, and vegan chocolate chips.

Cooking and Serving Tips

Chia pudding can be served warm or cold. To eat warm, heat in the microwave for 1 minute in a microwave-safe container.

## **Nutrition Facts**

- Calories 415
- Total Fat 22g 28%
- Saturated Fat 3g 15%
- Cholesterol 5mg 2%
- Sodium 168mg 7%
- Total Carbohydrate 40g 15%
- Dietary Fiber 17g 61%
- Total Sugars 20g
- Includes 6g Added Sugars 12%
- Protein 20g

# 47

# VEGAN RED CURRY LENTIL SOUP WITH KALE RECIPE

- Total Time: 50 min
- Prep Time: 10 min
- Cook Time: 40 min
- Servings: 6 (1 3/4 cups each)

This easy vegan lentil and kale soup is packed with rich flavor from red curry paste and coconut milk, which give an otherwise simple lentil soup a unique Southeast Asian spin. It's not over-powering or too spicy though, so the whole family can enjoy it, and it proves that meatless doesn't mean rabbit food. It's packed with unique flavor, from creamy coconut milk to a hint of Thai red curry paste.

Did you know vegan, vegetarian, and semi-vegetarian diets have been shown to help lower hemoglobin A1C? Cutting out or cutting back on meat may be intimidating to people with diabetes, as a plant-based diet limits protein options and tends to be higher in carbohydrate. However, eating more meatless meals will nudge you to eat more fruits, vegetables, whole grains, and beans, foods that are associated with an improved glycemic control. Plus, when carbohydrate comes in a fiber and nutrient-rich, unprocessed form, it can help stabilize blood sugar rather than spiking it.

## Ingredients

- 1 tablespoons extra-virgin olive oil
- 1 medium yellow onion, peeled and chopped
- 2 garlic cloves, peeled and minced
- 2 large carrots, peeled, trimmed, and chopped
- 1 ½ tablespoons red curry paste
- 1 14-ounce can low-sodium diced tomatoes
- 1 cup lentils, any color or mixture
- 4 cups low sodium vegetable broth
- ½ teaspoon salt
- ¼ teaspoon black pepper
- 4 cups chopped kale
- 1 cup reduced fat coconut milk

## Preparation

Heat olive oil in a large pot on medium-high heat. When hot, add onion, garlic, and carrots. Saute until onion is translucent, about 5 minutes.

Stir in red curry paste and cook until fragrant, about 1 minute.

Pour in diced tomatoes, lentils, broth, salt, and black pepper. Bring to a boil, then add kale. Cover soup, reduce heat to medium, and simmer 20 to 30 minutes, stirring occasionally, until lentils are tender.

Remove lid and stir in coconut milk. Heat through for 2 to 3 minutes then serve hot.

Ingredient Variations and Substitutions

If you prefer meat in your meals you could easily bump up the protein content with a little bit of ground turkey. Add 8 to 12 ounces of ground turkey after sauteing the vegetables along with the red curry paste, then cook until the meat is browned. If you'd like to add more protein while still keeping it meatless, stir in cubes of seasoned baked tofu at the end of cooking.

Cooking and Serving Tips

To find red curry paste, look in the Asian food aisle of your local grocery store. If you can't find it, feel free to swap green or yellow curry paste, or use a teaspoon of curry powder. Coconut milk is usually found in the Asian food aisle as well.

This recipe is easy to freeze, so I love to double up the ingredients and cook an extra batch. Store individual servings of soup in a plastic or glass container in the freezer and defrost for an easy dinner after a long day at work, or bring a few into the office for a homemade frozen meal.

If you have higher carbohydrate needs, serve this soup with another carbohydrate source. Try half a baked sweet potato or fruit salad—mango drizzled with lime juice and a pinch of red pepper flakes is a refreshing sweet and tart counterbalance with the rich soup. Or, if you eat less carbohydrate, serve this soup with a simple side salad topped with toasted cashews and a vinaigrette.

**Nutrition Facts**

- Calories 232
- Total Fat 8g 10%
- Saturated Fat 4g 20%
- Cholesterol 0mg 0%
- Sodium 452mg 20%
- Total Carbohydrate 31g 11%

- Dietary Fiber 10g 36%
- Total Sugars 7g
- Includes 0g Added Sugars 0%
- Protein 12g

# 48

# MEXICAN CHICKEN VERDE QUINOA CASSEROLE RECIPE

- Total Time: 90 min
- Prep Time: 30 min
- Cook Time: 60 min
- Servings: 6 (2 cups each)

This cheesy Mexican **q**uinoa casserole is a crowd pleaser! With 10 grams of fiber and 34 grams of protein per serving, it's a stick to your ribs kind of meal. Better yet, it's made in only one dish to minimize cleanup.

Besides the fact that this recipe is easy, delicious, and only re**q**uires a casserole dish, knife, and cutting board to prepare, one of my favorite things about this dish is just how easy it is to adapt to a variety of tastes and dietary needs. See all of the suggestions below.

### Ingredients

- 1 pound chicken breast (chopped into bite-sized pieces)
- 1 cup quinoa (rinsed)
- 2 cups black beans (canned, drained and rinsed)
- 2 medium yellow squash (or zucchini, chopped)
- 8 ounces mushrooms (quartered)
- 1 (4-ounce) can green chilies (drained)
- 3/4 cup salsa verde
- 1 tablespoon chili powder
- 1 1/2 teaspoons cumin
- 1/4 teaspoon salt
- 1/4 teaspoon black pepper
- 1 1/2 cups chicken broth (low-sodium)
- 2 cups peppers and onions (frozen)
- 1 cup jack cheese (grated)
- Optional: avocado, hot sauce, cilantro, and green onions for serving

### Preparation

Preheat oven to 375 F.

Spray a large casserole dish with oil. In the dish, mix together chicken, quinoa, black beans, yellow squash, mushrooms, chiles, salsa, spices, salt, and pepper.

Pour broth over the top, which helps move the quinoa to the bottom to cook through. Top with frozen peppers and onions.

Cover and place in the oven for 30 minutes. Remove lid and sprinkle cheese over the top. Place back in the oven and bake for another 30 minutes.

Let sit for 10 minutes so the liquids can finish absorbing, then serve with desired garnishes.

Ingredient Variations and Substitutions

Quinoa, the fiber-rich South American pseudo grain, makes

the perfect base for this casserole. It bakes up perfectly tender in the oven with just a little bit of chicken broth. Most grocery stores sell quinoa, but if you can't find it or aren't sure if you'll like it swap in brown rice.

If you use brown rice, top it with 2 cups of very hot chicken broth before baking and keep the casserole covered the whole time in the oven, as brown rice takes a bit longer to cook. When the rice is tender, sprinkle the casserole with cheese and place back in the oven another 5 minutes to melt.

For a meatless version, swap the chicken for cubes of tofu, crumbled tempeh, or add more beans. Try a mix of pinto beans and black beans for variety. Alternately, if your carbohydrate needs are lower, feel free to leave out the black beans and use an extra half pound of chicken.

Consider this *q*uinoa casserole recipe a template and play with a variety of different flavor combinations. Turn it into a Mediterranean *q*uinoa casserole by swapping in canned tomatoes for the salsa and chilies, use oregano, basil, and crushed red chili flakes for spices, white beans instead of black, and a sprinkle of feta before serving. Or try a broccoli cheddar version, leaving out the salsa and chilies, swapping broccoli for s*q*uash, cheddar for jack cheese, and use a teaspoon of dried thyme to flavor.

Cooking and Serving Tips

If you've ever cooked *q*uinoa before only to discover it had a slightly bitter taste, the problem may have been forgetting to rinse it. Quinoa comes coated with saponin, a naturally occurring chemical that helps it ward off insects. However, we humans don't like the bitter taste either, so make sure to give your *q*uinoa a good rinse in a fine mesh sieve before cooking.

Don't worry too much if you pull your casserole out of the oven and notice a little extra li*q*uid bubbling. Most of it will soak up while it sits. You may want to check the casserole towards the end of cooking. If it looks dry, add an extra *q*uarter cup of broth.

This recipe makes a fairly complete meal, but if you'd like something more substantial, try a serving of tortilla chips or a crunchy salad of romaine, radishes, and tomatoes with a lime vinaigrette.

## Nutrition Facts

- Calories 395
- Total Fat 11g 14%
- Saturated Fat 5g 25%
- Cholesterol 64mg 21%
- Sodium 697mg 30%
- Total Carbohydrate 43g 16%
- Dietary Fiber 10g 36%
- Total Sugars 7g
- Includes 0g
- Added Sugars 0%
- Protein 34g

# 49

# GLUTEN-FREE BREAKFAST CASSEROLE RECIPE

- Total Time: 50 min
- Prep Time: 25 min
- Cook Time: 25 min
- Servings: 8

Every brunch menu should include a simple one-dish recipe. This breakfast casserole is made with eggs, chicken sausage, cheese, and fresh tomato to create a hearty, protein-rich, healthy gluten-free breakfast. Assemble the ingredients ahead of time and bake just before company arrives or the family gets up to start their day. Leftovers are perfect for a brown bag lunch.

## Ingredients

- 5 slices gluten-free bread
- 5 links breakfast style chicken sausage
- 6 large eggs
- ½ cup half and half
- ¼ cup fresh basil leaves
- ¾ teaspoon kosher salt
- freshly ground black pepper to taste
- 1 cup cheddar cheese, shredded
- 1 large tomato, chopped

## Preparation

Preheat oven to 350F.

Spray a 9x9 square baking dish with nonstick spray.

Toast slices of bread. Once cool enough to handle dice into large pieces.

If sausage is frozen, thaw in the microwave or skillet according to package directions and then roughly chop.

Evenly distribute bread and sausage in the bottom of the prepared baking dish and set aside.

Combine eggs, half and half, and basil to blender; season with salt and pepper.

Blend for 30 seconds.

Pour egg mixture into prepared dish.

Sprinkle with cheese and tomato.

Carefully place in the oven and bake for 20 to 25 minutes or until eggs are set.

Remove from the oven and allow to cool for at least 15 minutes before serving.

Ingredient Variations and Substitutions

Replace basil with any fresh green herb such as parsley, chives, or tarragon. Swiss cheese and broccoli are just as delicious as cheddar and tomato.

Do your best to stick to the cup of cheese to keep the fat and calories in check.

Cooking and Serving Tips

To see if the eggs are cooked, press down gently on the top of the casserole and make sure no liquid egg runs out. If the top of the casserole begins to look too brown before the eggs are cooked through, cover the casserole loosely with aluminum foil for the remainder of cook time.

## Nutrition Facts

- Calories 222
- Total Fat 15g 19%
- Saturated Fat 7g 35%
- Cholesterol 183mg 61%
- Sodium 519mg 23%
- Total Carbohydrate 11g 4%
- Dietary Fiber 1g 4%
- Total Sugars 3g
- Includes 0g
- Added Sugars 0%
- Protein 12g

# 50

# GRAIN-FREE STRAWBERRY GRANOLA

- Total Time: 35 min
- Prep Time: 15 min
- Cook Time: 20 min
- Servings: 24 (1/4 cup each)

Whether you're following a lower carb lifestyle or simply in need of a celiac disease friendly snack, this grain-free granola is easy to make and downright addictive.

Granola without grains can easily be confused as glorified trail mix—unless you know the secret. The trick to perfectly crunchy clusters is chopping the ingredients in a good processor for a few short pulses before a **q**uick toast in the oven.

## Ingredients

- 2 tablespoons coconut oil
- ¼ cup honey
- ½ teaspoon coarse sea salt
- 1 teaspoon vanilla extract
- 1 cup raw almonds
- 1 cup raw shelled pistachios
- 1 cup unsweetened coconut chips
- 1 cup shelled pumpkin seeds
- 1 cup freeze dried strawberries

### Preparation
Preheat oven to 300F.

Line a baking sheet with parchment paper and set aside.

Place coconut oil in a microwave safe bowl and microwave for about 30 sections, until melted.

In a medium sized bowl mix melted coconut oil, honey, salt, and vanilla and whisk well to combine.

In a food processor combine almonds, pistachios, coconut chips and pumpkin seeds; pulse about 10 times to roughly chop.

Pour contents of food processor into bowl with honey mixture and then toss to coat.

Transfer mixture to prepared baking sheet and spread in an even layer.

Bake, stirring occasionally, until golden brown (15 to 20 minutes). Remove from oven. Once completely cool, mix in strawberries. Store in an airtight container for up to two weeks.

Ingredient Variations and Substitutions

For an extra boost of flavor add half a teaspoon of ground cardamom, turmeric, or cinnamon to the honey mixture. You can also experiment with the colors and flavors of various types of freeze dried fruit.

Cooking and Serving Tips

Keep an eye on the granola towards the end of cooking to be sure the edges don't burn; proper mixing periodically during baking will also help prevent this from happening.

Be sure that the mixture is completely cool before adding the freeze dried fruit, otherwise it can get soggy.

For easier honey pouring, coat your measuring container with a single spray of oil (or grease it with just a drop of oil) before adding the honey. It'll help the honey slide right out into the bowl.

**Nutrition Facts**

- Calories 175
- Total Fat 14g 18%
- Saturated Fat 5g 25%
- Cholesterol 0mg 0%
- Sodium 74mg 3%
- Total Carbohydrate 9g 3%
- Dietary Fiber 2g 7%
- Total Sugars 4g
- Includes 3g Added Sugars 6%
- Protein 6g

## 51

# BLACK BEAN-ARUGULA TOSTADAS WITH TURMERIC GUACAMOLE

- Total Time: 20 min
- Prep Time: 10 min
- Cook Time: 10 min
- Servings: 2 (2 tostadas each)

Eating more plant-based meals can help boost your intake of antioxidants, fiber, and vitamins and minerals. Here's a flavorful, meatless version of a Mexican classic.

These tacos feature black beans, which have high levels of a potent antioxidant called anthocyanins, thanks to their darkly pigmented skins. That's not where the anti-inflammatory, antioxidant benefits end—the turmeric in the guacamole is also a potent antioxidant. In addition, the beans contribute fiber and iron while the avocado delivers healthy monounsaturated fat. This protein-fat combo keeps you satisfied longer—much longer than it'll take you to whip up this recipe.

**Ingredients**

- 4 6-inch whole grain corn tortillas
- 1.5 tablespoons olive oil
- 2 cups canned black beans, rinsed and drained
- 1/2 cup salsa
- 1/2 medium avocado, peeled and diced
- 1 tablespoon finely chopped red onion
- 1 medium clove garlic
- 1 teaspoon fresh lemon juice
- 1/4 teaspoon powdered turmeric
- 1/4 teaspoon ground cumin
- 1/8 teaspoon salt
- pinch of ground black pepper
- 4 cups arugula
- 1/2 cup chopped tomato
- 1/4 teaspoon red pepper flakes (optional)

**Preparation**

Preheat the oven to 350F.

Brush 2 teaspoons of olive oil over both sides of each tortilla, place on a baking sheet, and bake until crispy, about 10 minutes.

In a blender, pulse beans and salsa until about half the beans are pureed and half remain chunky. Add water, 1 tablespoon at a time, if you need to thin the mixture. If you prefer the beans warm instead of room temperature, heat in a microwave-safe dish for 1 minute, or until heated through.

In a medium bowl, mash the avocado, red onion, garlic, lemon juice, turmeric, cumin, salt, and pepper together until smooth.

Heat 2 tablespoons of water in a large pan and add the 4 cups of arugula, mixing until only slightly wilted, then remove from the water.

Assemble your tostada. Spread the bean and salsa mixture on the baked tortilla and top with the wilted arugula, chopped tomato, guacamole, and sprinkle of red pepper flake.

Ingredient Variations and Substitutions

If you're not a fan of or just don't have black beans handy, use pinto beans or kidney beans instead. Or, try a version with garbanzo beans and use curry powder in the guacamole in place of turmeric and cumin. You'll still receive the filling fiber, iron, and antioxidants.

Fresh sprouts, like sunflower sprouts, can replace the arugula if you prefer a crunchier, uncooked topping. In fact, you can use kale or spinach instead of the arugula if you're not a fan of the taste.

Want to make this dish a burrito bowl? Swap the tortilla out for cooked quinoa or brown rice. Substitute lime in for lemon to add a slightly different flavor profile and swap in chili powder in place of cumin to add a mild kick.

Cooking and Serving Tips

Let the garlic sit for 10 minutes after you mince it and your body will absorb more of the active antioxidant compounds.

Corn tortilla freeze well and thaw quickly, so store extras in the freezer if you don't plan to use them within a week.

You can tell an avocado is ripe when it's stem falls easily away and leaves a patch of bright green flesh exposed.

If you like softer tortillas, brush with oil and heat in a skillet until just warm.

**Nutrition Facts**

- Calories 461
- Total Fat 14g 18%
- Saturated Fat 2g 10%
- Cholesterol 0mg 0%
- Sodium 784mg 34%

- Total Carbohydrate 70g 25%
- Dietary Fiber 21g 75%
- Total Sugars 3g
- Includes 0g Added Sugars 0%
- Protein 19g

# 52

## MEDITERRANEAN SPICED SWORDFISH WITH TOMATO OLIVE BRUSCHETTA

- Total Time: 45 min
- Prep Time: 15 min
- Cook Time: 30 min
- Servings: 4

Bruschetta is a classic Italian antipasto, or appetizer. It is traditionally made of tomatoes and served over grilled bread. This version has the addition of olives, which add a tanginess to the bruschetta as well as heart-healthy monounsaturated fat.

Swordfish are native to the Mediterranean Sea as well as much of the Atlantic, Pacific, and Indian oceans. They are very large fish, often growing to be well over 200 lbs. Swordfish are an excellent source of protein, however, consumption should be limited since their large size typically meals a higher mercury content.


## Ingredients

- 2 large white potatoes
- 4 tablespoons olive oil (divided)
- 1 3/4 teaspoon salt (divided)
- 1 1/2 teaspoon black pepper (divided)
- 1/2 teaspoon paprika
- 1½ cups tomatoes, diced (I used roma tomatoes)
- 2/3 cup kalamata olives, diced
- 8 fresh basil leaves, thinly sliced
- 1 scallion, chopped
- 3 cloves garlic (divided)
- 1 pound swordfish
- 1 teaspoon ground coriander
- 1 teaspoon ground cumin
- 1/2 teaspoon sweet Spanish paprika
- 3 cups green beans, raw
- 1 tablespoon lemon juice

## Preparation
Preheat oven to 400F.

Wash potatoes and cut into wedges. Toss with 2 tablespoons of olive oil, 1/2 teaspoon of salt, 1/2 teaspoon black pepper, and 1/2 teaspoon paprika. Bake for 30 minutes, flipping halfway through.

While the potatoes are cooking, chop your tomatoes, olives, basil, and scallions. Mince the garlic. Mix in 1 tablespoon olive oil, garlic, 1/2 teaspoon salt, and 1/4 teaspoon black pepper. Refrigerate until ready to serve.

Heat a large nonstick skillet over medium-high heat. Pat

swordfish dry with a paper towel. Sprinkle both sides with 1/2 teaspoon salt, coriander, 1/2 teaspoon black pepper, cumin, and Spanish parika and rub to evenly distribute. Coat pan with cooking spray. Cook fish on high heat for 4 minutes on each side. Add a small amount of water to the pan if it starts to smoke.

Place green beans in a microwave safe bowl with a few tablespoons of water. Cover with plastic wrap, leaving a small slit for steam. Microwave for 3 minutes. Once cooked, remove the plastic wrap and toss with 1 tablespoon olive oil, lemon juice, 1 clove of garlic, 1/4 teaspoon salt, and 1/4 teaspoon black pepper.

Divide green beans, potatoes, and swordfish evenly among 4 plates. Top swordfish with bruschetta.

Ingredient Variations and Substitutions

Tuna steaks also work well in this recipe.

Asparagus is a good substitute if you do not like green beans.

Cooking and Serving Tips

If you're having a tough time peeling the garlic clove, here's a little trick: Place it down flat on your cutting, place the wide portion of your knife over it, and gently crush it. After this, the peel should come right off.

**Nutrition Facts**

- Calories 464
- Total Fat 22g 28%
- Saturated Fat 4g 20%
- Cholesterol 44mg 15%
- Sodium 1338mg 58%
- Total Carbohydrate 41g 15%
- Dietary Fiber 9g 32%
- Total Sugars 5g
- Includes 0g
- Added Sugars 0%
- Protein 29g

# 53

# CHERRY BERRY ANTI-INFLAMMATORY SMOOTHIE BOWL

- Total Time: 7 min
- Prep Time: 7 min
- Cook Time: 0 min
- Servings: 2

If you've never had a smoothie bowl, you're in for a treat. It's a thicker, creamier version of a smoothie you can eat with a spoon, like soft-serve ice cream.

Cherries and berries are the antioxidant-rich stars of this cold and creamy smoothie bowl recipe. You'll get a boost of inflammation-fighting antioxidants from them, plus crunchy texture and nutrition in the toppings.

## Ingredients

- ½ cup 2% milk
- 1 cup low-fat plain yogurt
- 1 cup frozen mixed berries
- 1 cup frozen cherries (any variety, such as black, Barbados, or Mount Ranier)
- 1 cup grated carrots
- 2 tablespoons sliced almonds
- 1 tablespoon almond butter
- 1 tablespoon fresh lemon juice
- 1 medium kiwi, sliced
- 1 tablespoon chia seeds
- 1 tablespoon unsweetened coconut flakes

## Preparation

Combine milk, yogurt, berries, cherries, carrots, almonds, almond butter, and lemon juice in a blender. Blend on high until smooth, adding water as needed to thin the mixture.

Split between two bowls and top each with kiwi slices, chia seeds, and coconut flakes.

Ingredient Variations and Substitutions

The beauty of smoothie bowls is that they can be customized to the season, and to your preferences. Swap in one type of fruit for another in equal amounts, replace almond butter with an equal amount of a different type of nut or seed butter (peanut butter, cashew butter, sunflower seed butter), and replace the other healthy fats like nuts or coconut in equal amounts.

Get creative by adding your favorite spices and garnishing with mint, basil, or any other herb. You can increase the potassium in the smoothie bowl by swapping banana for cherries, berries, or kiwi.

Cooking and Serving Tips

Prep-ahead tip: Pre-measure the fruit and veggies and place in a freezer safe bag or container in the serving amount desired. Label the bag with the name of the smoothie bowl, and the ingredients left to add in their amounts (i.e. "add 1 cup 2% milk, 1 cup low-fat plain yogurt, 1 tablespoon almond butter, 1 tablespoon lemon juice). You won't have to measure as much in the morning, or look-up the recipe!

Using frozen berries and cherries not only gives this smoothie bowl the right consistency (the fruit acts as ice to make the smoothie cold and creamy), it also allows you to have nutrient-rich berries picked at the peak of ripeness (meaning they also have the most nutrition) all year long.

If you don't have a high-powered blender, add the frozen fruit and milk together in half portions at a time until blended. This will make it easier to get a smooth consistency. Add water as needed to thin the mixture if it's too thick.

And for a fun treat, freeze the smoothie bowl ingredients in ice pop moulds (stir the toppings in) to create ice pops!

**Nutrition Facts**

- Calories 337
- Total Fat 12g 15%
- Saturated Fat 4g 20%
- Cholesterol 12mg 4%
- Sodium 199mg 9%
- Total Carbohydrate 48g 17%
- Dietary Fiber 10g 36%
- Total Sugars 31g
- Includes 1g Added Sugars 2%
- Protein 14g

# 54

# MEDITERRANEAN SPINACH TURKEY MEATBALLS WITH VEGETABLE ORZO

- Total Time: 50 min
- Prep Time: 25 min
- Cook Time: 25 min
- Servings: 4

Although it's shaped like rice, orzo is actually a type of pasta. It cooks much faster than rice, making it a great choice in a soup or a quick side dish. This recipe uses whole wheat orzo which provides 30 grams of whole grains per serving. Bell peppers are a great source of vitamin C, which functions as an antioxidant and plays a role in immune function. Whole grains, vegetables, lean

IRMA LOPEZ

protein such as turkey, and heart-healthy fats such as olive oil are pinnacles of the Mediterranean diet.

**Ingredients**

- 2 cups baby spinach
- 3 garlic cloves (or 1½ teaspoon minced garlic)
- 1 pound ground turkey
- 1 egg
- 1 cup mozzarella cheese, shredded
- ½ tablespoon basil, dried
- 1 tablespoon oregano, dried
- 1/4 teaspoon salt
- 1/4 teaspoon pepper
- 1/2 cup panko breadcrumbs
- 3/4 cup whole wheat orzo, dry
- 1 red bell pepper, chopped
- 1 yellow bell pepper, chopped
- 1/2 red onion, chopped
- 2 tablespoons olive oil
- 1 tablespoon lemon juice
- ½ cup fresh basil
- 1/4 teaspoon sea salt
- 1/8 teaspoon black pepper

**Preparation**

Put baby spinach and garlic in your food processor. Pulse into very small pieces. If you don't have a food processor, dice until spinach and garlic are very finely chopped.

Mix turkey, egg, cheese, spinach and garlic mixture, basil, oregano, salt, pepper, and the breadcrumbs into a large mixing bowl.

Form into about 16 meatballs. You may need to add a little more breadcrumbs if mixture is too wet to form. Bake meatballs for 20-25 minutes at 400F.

Bring a large pot of water to a boil. Once boiling, add the orzo and cook for 8 to 9 minutes. Drain in a colander. Put back into the pot and mix well with olive oil to prevent it from sticking.

While the orzo is cooking, dice your peppers and onion into small pieces if you haven't already done so. Slice basil into thin strips.

Add peppers, onion, garlic, lemon juice, fresh basil, salt, and pepper in with the orzo. Mix well.

Serve meatballs over a bed of orzo.

Ingredient Variations and Substitutions

Ground chicken works just as well in this recipe.

Vegetables in the orzo can also be substituted based on what you have on hand. Tomatoes or carrots would also work well.

Cooking and Serving Tips

If you're having a tough time peeling the garlic clove, here's a little trick: Place it down flat on your cutting board, place the wide portion of your knife over it, and gently crush it. After this, the peel should come right off.

You can form into as many meatballs as you want, but this cooking time is appropriate for 16 meatballs (1 ounce of turkey each).

**Nutrition Facts**

- Calories 550
- Total Fat 25g 32%
- Saturated Fat 7g 35%
- Cholesterol 146mg 49%
- Sodium 527mg 23%
- Total Carbohydrate 46g 17%
- Dietary Fiber 7g 25%
- Total Sugars 3g
- Includes 0g Added Sugars 0%
- Protein 38g

# 55

# LOADED MEDITERRANEAN SALAD WITH CAULIFLOWER TABBOULEH

- Total Time: 35 min
- Prep Time: 25 min
- Cook Time: 10 min
- Servings: 4

Tabbouleh is a traditional Mediterranean grain salad that's typically made with bulgur, tomatoes, onion, and parsley, among a few other ingredients. This version is lightened up with riced cauliflower, which provides a similar consistency to bulgur but offers a lower carb and calorie count. The tabbouleh can also be eaten by itself, in a wrap, or as a dip with pita chips.

The Mediterranean diet emphasizes whole grains, vegetables, and healthy fats, which have been shown to help optimize cholesterol levels in the blood. This recipe incorporates those components with whole wheat couscous, olive oil, walnuts, and several servings of vegetables. The moderate portion feta cheese adds rich flavor and classic Mediterranean taste.

**Ingredients**

- 1/2 cup whole wheat couscous (dry)
- 1 1/3 cup riced cauliflower
- 1 cup cherry tomatoes
- ½ cup white onion
- 1 cup fresh parsley
- ½ cup scallions
- 15 mint leaves
- 2 tablespoons olive oil
- 1 tablespoon lemon juice
- ½ teaspoon salt
- ¼ teaspoon black pepper
- Arugula, or other small leafy green of your choice
- 4 ounces feta cheese (1 cup)
- 1 can low sodium chickpeas
- 1 cup cucumber (half of a large cucumber)
- 2 ounces shelled walnuts (1/2 cup)
- 4 tablespoons balsamic vinegar

**Preparation**

Start by making the tabbouleh (steps 1-3). Cook couscous according to package directions, omitting any butter/oil/salt.

While couscous is cooking, chop your vegetables and herbs. Quarter the cherry tomatoes. Chop the onion into fine pieces.

Mix couscous, riced cauliflower, tomatoes, onion, parsley, scallions, and mint in a large bowl. Add olive oil and lemon juice. Season with salt and pepper.

Fill a large salad bowl with arugula, then cucumbers and

tabbouleh. Sprinkle feta cheese and walnuts over the top. Drizzle with balsamic vinegar.

Ingredient Variations and Substitutions

Cauliflower florets can be riced at home. Just place the cauliflower florets into a food processor and pulse until completely broken down.

Feta cheese can be omitted to make this meal vegan.

Couscous can be replaced with quinoa to make it gluten-free.

Cooking and Servings Tips

Tabbouleh can also be made the day before and stored in the fridge. Flavors will meld together nicely overnight.

If you bought your couscous in bulk, without specified directions, bring ½ cup water to a boil. Once boiling, add the couscous, stir, and then turn off the heat. Cover and let couscous absorb the water for 5 minutes.

**Nutrition Facts**

- Calories 460
- Total Fat 25g 32%
- Saturated Fat 6g 30%
- Cholesterol 25mg 8%
- Sodium 738mg 32%
- Total Carbohydrate 46g 17%
- Dietary Fiber 10g 36%
- Total Sugars 11g
- Includes 0g
- Added Sugars 0%
- Protein 17g

CPSIA information can be obtained
at www.ICGtesting.com
Printed in the USA
BVHW092156200521
607797BV00004B/549

9 781802 836578